The
History
of the
Internet

For my parents, grandad and Angelika
And in memory of Yvonne Laws

The History of the Internet

In Byte-Sized Chunks

Chris Stokel-Walker

Michael O'Mara Books Limited

First published in Great Britain in 2023 by
Michael O'Mara Books Limited
9 Lion Yard
Tremadoc Road
London SW4 7NQ

'Requiem of the ARPANET' poem used with kind permission of Vint Cerf.

Every reasonable effort has been made to acknowledge all copyright holders. Any errors or omissions that may have occurred are inadvertent, and anyone with any copyright queries is invited to write to the publisher, so that a full acknowledgement may be included in subsequent editions of this work.

A CIP catalogue record for this book is available from the British Library.

This product is made of material from well-managed, FSC®-certified forests and other controlled sources. The manufacturing processes conform to the environmental regulations of the country of origin.

ISBN: 978-1-78929-559-7 in hardback print format
ISBN: 978-1-78929-594-8 in trade paperback format
ISBN: 978-1-78929-560-3 in ebook format

1 2 3 4 5 6 7 8 9 10

Cover design by Ana Bjezancevic
Designed and typeset by Design23
Cover picture credits: Shutterstock

Printed and bound by CPI Group (UK) Ltd, Croydon, CR0 4YY

www.mombooks.com

MIX
Paper | Supporting
responsible forestry
FSC® C171272

Contents

Introduction
A Day in the Life of the Internet

When's the first time in the day that you interact with the internet?

For many people, it'll be when they first pick up the mobile phone sat on their bedside table and scroll through emails, check their WhatsApp groups, or look for the latest social media updates.

It might be when you open a news app like the BBC's or CNN's and catch up on events that happened overnight. Or perhaps it's your morning burst of Duolingo – the glitzy, gamified language learning app that claims to be able to make you fluent if you give it enough attention. It could be a check of the weather, updates to which are beamed from any number of providers to your phone on demand. Maybe it's a quick scrub through a YouTube video as you try to linger a little longer in bed.

For a growing number, their first online interaction comes before all that. The burgeoning industry of the internet of things (IoT) – devices that are connected to the internet – means that the alarm clock that wakes you up, or the lights that slowly get brighter to try to ease you into the day in a modern mimicry of nature, could well be connected to the internet.

Whichever it is, one thing is for sure: for the overwhelming majority of you reading this book – for almost everyone except my resolutely analogue parents, who are happy with their chunky, unconnected mobile phone – you'll have an early morning interaction with the internet.

It's a story that repeats itself as the sun moves westwards across the planet, waking up one country then the next in its regular routine.

The internet never sleeps, even if you do. A constantly updating, ever-growing behemoth, there's always something happening online. That's natural when you consider that the internet is a rapidly expanding community of 5 billion people – and millions more bots and artificial intelligence-powered facsimiles of humankind – with new users logging on every day.

That's what makes it quite so addictive. There are close to 2 billion websites to explore, new shores on the constantly expanding map of charted territory that the average internet user is free to visit. And on those websites, there are new bits of content: millions of new videos on TikTok every day and hundreds of hours of new footage on YouTube every minute.

There are new tweets, new Facebook posts, new Instagram Stories. There are new comments on forums, on subreddits, within comment sections. There are new Google searches to be made and new Wikipedia pages to explore; new avenues of information to go down.

There are new emails to be read – a third of a trillion of them sent daily, by one estimate – and new chat messages to be consumed. There are new baby photos and memes to be viewed; new congratulations and commiserations to be sent and received.

Little wonder, then, that we are addicted. Our dopamine receptors are being spammed. There are always new things to be learned, new adventures to be had, new people to be met behind every profile picture, every post and every swipe right. There is always more.

Six in ten Britons cannot imagine their everyday lives anymore without the internet – roughly the same proportion as Nigerians, Swedes and Brazilians. (Americans are far more aloof: just 45 per cent say that it's unimaginable to be offline.)

This is the story of how we got to this point. It's the story of the unreal technology that delivers every bleep and buzz and blaring red notification icon to our ears and eyeballs. It's the history of the internet, and of everything we consume through it.

Some of these stories will be familiar to you. Others won't be. When dealing with something as large and ever-growing as the internet, you're bound to pick up a nugget of new information along the way – just as you're likely to encounter the same tired old meme you've seen circulating on Facebook for years now.

There'll also be bits missing. You can't sum up the history of the internet in a 224-page book without skipping some parts, even if you keep each entry as concise as it is comprehensive.

The size of Wikipedia at the start of 2023 was 4,349,234,241 (four billion, three hundred and forty-nine million, two hundred and thirty-four thousand, two hundred and forty-one) words. This book is 55,000 words long, or roughly one-one hundred thousandth of that number. Even in 2002, a little under a year into Wikipedia's existence (which we'll get onto later), the sum total of its word count was roughly one hundred times greater than this book's.

Yet this book tries to give shape to an always expanding, spreading blob of bits and bytes. It may seem a bit like herding cats (which the internet also likes), but it's an attempt to bring shape, form and solid factual information to the online world.

It tries to encapsulate what the internet is, where it came from, where it's going – and what it's doing to us – in as much detail as possible. The hope is to give you the curated, considered history of the internet, in bite – or byte – sized pieces.

Chapter 1
The Creation of the Internet

J. C. R. Licklider's dream

If you need a GPS or satnav system to traverse the nearly 2 billion websites online today, and the mountains more content being posted every single second to what we now know as the World Wide Web, things were far simpler at its genesis.

At the birth of the internet in 1969, to navigate this brave new world you only needed the four points of a compass. That's right: the vast internet we use today started off with just four possible destinations.

Fittingly, given the way that tech giants located in and around southern California have come to dominate the way we live our online lives in the twenty-first century, all four points of the internet's compass back in 1969 were also firmly rooted on or near the west coast of the United States.

To the north there was the Stanford Research Institute, located in Menlo Park, California. Around 750 miles east you'd find the University of Utah. At the southern point of the compass stood the University of California, Los Angeles (UCLA), while its westernmost expanse ended at the University of California-Santa Barbara, less than 100 miles west of UCLA.

Each of those destinations housed a computer. Because before the internet we know today, where users visit websites, things looked quite different. (The World Wide Web didn't even exist until 1989.) Instead, there were what were called 'network nodes' – computers to most of us – that computer-mad academics at each university wanted to link together.

Computers as we know them today had been around for a few decades before the late 1960s' birth of the internet, their development bolstered by the exigencies of the Second World War and the desire to decrypt enemy messages and calculate complicated equations to decide where, when and how to explode the new range of bombs that were being used against opponents. But they had been kept in isolation, within computational or engineering departments inside universities, where access to them was tightly monitored.

Still, it was post-war idealism that helped create the internet. MIT researcher J. C. R. Licklider first conceived of the idea of what he called a 'Galactic Network' in August 1962, where users at computers around the world would be able to access information held on an altogether different machine in a different part of the planet. Licklider's dream, which he outlined in a series of memos, would become the impetus for the internet we know and love (or hate) today.

ARPANET: The internet's military history

Two months later, in October 1962, Licklider would become the first head of the computer research programme at the Defense Advanced Research Projects Agency, or DARPA, the US Department of Defense's research and development agency.

The internet's history is steeped in its time and its military connections: tests within the United States government and military apparatus about how it would respond to a consequential nuclear strike from the Soviet Union found that the way the country's command and control network was established was sorely lacking. A nuclear bomb from the Soviet Union detonating above the United States would knock out FM radio networks for hours; a handful of strikes on land could destroy AT&T's nationwide telephone network. An alternative was needed for the country's safety. Money would be thrown at the problem, with the goal of creating a less centralized communication network that would not be susceptible to being taken offline by a single surgical strike – or the brute force of a hydrogen bomb.

'He had a philosophy that is not often acknowledged,' Leonard Kleinrock, one of the computer scientists brought in to work on the ARPANET project, which brought the internet into existence in the 1960s, told me. Kleinrock is a member of the Internet Hall of Fame and remains, at almost ninety, a vibrant raconteur, telling stories about the early days of the internet. Kleinrock's own few chapters in the history of the internet include coming up with a key contribution to the idea of queueing theory, which even today helps transfer data from one computer to another.

Licklider's approach to funding was a simple one, Kleinrock explained. 'He provided funding in a way that instilled and inspired innovation and creativity,' he said. Licklider would give researchers piles of money, no questions asked, to pursue their goals. 'Shoot for the moon,' Kleinrock recalled Licklider saying to him and others. 'Do something enormous and significant that you couldn't have done without this nice funding.' It came with no strings attached. The funding for the plan to develop what was called the 'Intergalactic Computer Network' was as significant as the vision Licklider had: 'It seems to me to be interesting and important … to develop a capability for integrated network operation,' he wrote to the team he put together.

Kleinrock says that funding without caveats allowed the internet to blossom in its earliest days of conception. Licklider set up and supported centres of excellence around the country that each specialized in areas of science that the US Department of Defense wanted to bring together in order to pool expertise.

But that was easier said than done. The idea of sharing knowledge, and computing power in university computer departments, was unheard of. Each university was extremely territorial, and they were wary of sharing their resources with each other. In part, that was because the idea of networking computers together to share resources had never been done. But Licklider managed to convince – some might say strong-arm – researchers in universities across the country to take part.

College campus computers

These early computers, which would often fill entire rooms of college buildings, were seen as a major boon for students trying to tackle key problems in mathematics-based fields, such as physics. Their prowess at procedurally calculating difficult equations meant that they could outpace the humans – often highly skilled, underpaid women 'computers' (who computed things) – from whom the devices borrowed their name.

But there was just one problem: they were finickity to work with and prone to going wrong. They were also expensive and complicated feats of engineering; colleges didn't always want their students getting unfettered access to them and playing about with their innards. Demand was also high, which meant that universities' computing departments began trying to separate users from the computers themselves to limit arguments.

The room-filling computers, which had a tiny fraction of the power of today's devices, could only operate a single program at a time, and not at all interactively. Instead, high priests of computing – called operators – would feed pre-prepared punch cards into the machines. The holes in each punch card provided instructions to the computer. Get one hole in the wrong place and your program could fail, giving you nothing back – not that you'd know until ages later, once your punch card had been processed.

It wasn't a viable solution in the long term, so over time techniques developed that enabled users to connect directly to computers and for users to share time on the computer using a round-robin approach. It gave the impression of real-time access. And it got rid of the high priests acting as a conduit between users and the computer.

The way they did this was by installing terminals onto campuses. These monitors and keyboards were remote from the large core computers but allowed users to type a command into the terminal, which would then be transmitted and calculated by the computer when it could.

There was, of course, a different way: one proposed by Licklider, and one he put into action through ARPANET.

The first message on the internet

The sickly green walls of room 3420 in Boelter Hall, the home of UCLA's engineering department, might not seem like the site of a world-changing moment – but it was, on 29 October 1969. It was the moment that a project signed off by ARPA (formerly DARPA), to develop a four-node network that could connect computers at each site to one another, would become a reality. Given the project had been allocated an initial budget of $563,000 in 1968, the equivalent of $4.6 million today, making sure it went well was important.

Charlie Kline, a student of Kleinrock at UCLA, was sat at a computer terminal in room 3420 that was connected to ARPANET. That sounds grandiose, but the reality is more prosaic: it was a connection between the computer at UCLA and one staffed by Bill Duvall, a similarly junior engineer at the Stanford Research Institute.

Neither the UCLA nor Stanford engineers were too sure their plan to send a message from a computer in one location to another, 350 miles north-west, would work. So, they created a telephone link between Kline and Duvall to ensure that if things went wrong with the computers, there'd be a way to salvage the experiment.

Sure enough, it was needed. Kline, based at UCLA, typed the letters L and O into his computer – the start of the command 'login', that would allow him to log into the computer based in Stanford. But the G didn't arrive. UCLA's computer had crashed.

The first message sent over the internet, at 10.30 p.m. on 29 October 1969, as recorded in a lined notebook kept alongside the UCLA machine to act as a record of everything that happened on the device, was therefore 'Lo'.

'As in "lo and behold",' said Kleinrock. The message came from failure but was a boon. 'We couldn't have asked for a more powerful, more succinct, more prophetic message than "lo".'

The notebook in which news of the first message being sent was documented – as 'talked to SRI host to host' – was one stolen from Scientific Data Systems, according to Kleinrock. That simple message, sent from one site to another, was a proof of concept, and one that would establish a new norm of communication. Even if it did crash partway through. And it came just fifteen weeks after humans landed on the moon for the first time – an indication of how revolutionary that period was.

At the time, Kleinrock and his colleagues would have had little idea of how important what they had done would become. But they did have some sense of what their technical demonstration had unlocked. To mark the occasion, UCLA published a press release announcing what had happened on that October evening. In it, Kleinrock said this:

> As of now, computer networks are still in their infancy. But as they grow up and become more sophisticated, we will probably see the spread of 'computer utilities', which, like present electric and telephone utilities, will service individual homes and offices across the country.

The internet was born. And like any newborn, it would grow quickly. That first connection took place between UCLA and Stanford in late October 1969. By December, all four nodes on the initial project had been hooked up. By April 1971, it became fifteen nodes – though good luck getting access to the nascent internet in flyover country in the United States: nodes were concentrated on both coasts, with little in between.

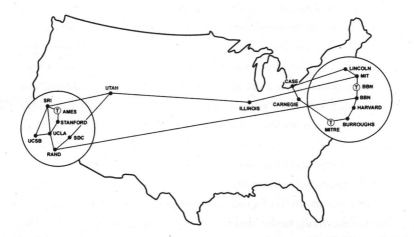

The map of ARPANET, as of September 1971.

Still, things were moving – fast. By June 1973, a Norwegian seismic data collection facility near Oslo, called NORSAR, was linked up to ARPANET. The following month, a computer at University College London was connected to ARPANET, also using NORSAR – and would soon be outmoded by a satellite connection linking across the Atlantic.

The internet spreads

From there, the internet began to expand, with disparate, separate networks connecting to each other, bit by bit. Think of it like a spider weaving its web: at first you see one strand connecting from point to point, then another criss-crosses it. NORSAR in Norway was the gateway into Europe, where various networks began to spring up.

Communicating using this new technology was one initial problem overcome by Ray Tomlinson, the inventor of email. Before Tomlinson's brainwave in 1971 that would eventually become email, users of ARPANET could only leave messages for one another on the same computers – more accurately described as Interface Message Processors, or IMPs – they were working on. (A fun historical footnote is that the first IMP, used to send the 'Lo' message, operated for 7,792 hours before being replaced.) If someone used a different IMP, you couldn't necessarily communicate with them. That was an issue given the growing scale of ARPANET: at the time there were around twenty machines connected in the United States, and each had up to fifty users. So you might want to communicate with one of 1,000 or more people, but couldn't easily.

Tomlinson, an MIT graduate, like many saw this as a problem. But unlike many, he decided to come up with a solution. You could direct the IMP to send a message to another IMP by typing in the destination: the username of whoever you wanted to send it to and the name of the computer they used, separated by an @ symbol. (The @ symbol was chosen because it was deemed unlikely to ever be present in a person's name.) It was a move that would have massive ramifications, but emails might not have been so widely used were it not for the advocacy of Stephen Lukasik, a director at ARPA at the time, who told staff that the most effective way to contact him was to use the nascent tool. People did: Lukasik became swamped by a deluge of email; by 1976, a study conducted by ARPA found that 75 per cent of all the traffic on ARPANET was due to email.

In part that was because of another innovation that piggybacked on the new technology: discussion groups. In 1975, Steve Walker, an ARPA manager, suggested the idea and it was taken up by a handful of users.

By 1974, the word 'internet' was first being used to describe this network of networks, coined by Vint Cerf, a computer scientist working at Stanford University at the time (though in his paper 'A Protocol for Packet Network Intercommunication', he uses the longer 'internetwork'). The 1970s saw more research-forward universities sign up to the internet, and Queen Elizabeth II sent her first email on 26 March 1976, from the Royal Signals and Radar Establishment in Malvern, England. She used the username HME2 – Her Majesty Elizabeth II – and was under the supervision of Peter Kirstein, who was the driving force that helped set up the first UK node for ARPANET in 1973.

Even with the Queen's support, though, things weren't ready to go stratospheric for the internet just yet. The real explosion came in the 1980s, thanks to a grant provided by the US National Science Foundation (NSF), which established the Computer Science Network (CSNET). This allowed smaller, less well-funded universities to connect to ARPANET. Launched in 1981, CSNET's mission was to be self-sufficient within five years. It achieved that: by 1984, more than 180 university departments were part of CSNET. The reasons were obvious: it was far cheaper to get onto CSNET that it was ARPANET. Connections to ARPANET required the installation and maintenance of equipment that would cost around $100,000 or more every year, something that around nine in every ten university computer science departments in the US couldn't afford. Access to CSNET could be arranged at around a fifth of the cost of ARPANET, in part because it was focused much more on email exchange, which made it cheaper.

And while the internet became more academic and less military, the armed forces splintered off into their own section of the internet: MILNET (Military Network) assured its users more secure communications away from the prying eyes of the academy. In all, sixty-eight out of the 113 ARPANET nodes that existed at the time were shunted over to MILNET, where no one else could access them.

CSNET bequeaths NSFNET

Given the success of CSNET, thoughts moved on not just to how to make access to the internet more equal in academia, but to how to spread it more widely. In 1985, the NSF (National Science Foundation) built a range of supercomputers (high-powered, high-end computers) and sought to ensure that scientists around the country could harness their power to make calculations. So, they connected them to the internet. The speed at which data could be sent and received from the NSF supercomputers was a blistering 56,000 bits per second (or 56k) – which would be a standard internet connection speed for dial-up modems more than ten years later.

In 1986, NSFNET, the NSF's version of ARPANET, was born: it used TCP/IP protocols, which were used for sending packets of data from one destination to another over the internet and had been adopted as standard by ARPANET on 1 January 1983. TCP/IP was invented by Vint Cerf and Bob Kahn at DARPA, with the science behind the protocol published in a December 1974 academic paper. Until TCP/IP's adoption, the number of different computer networks that were operating on the internet around the world didn't have the ability to communicate across networks: if you were on a non-ARPANET network, for instance, prior to 1983 you couldn't communicate with a computer on ARPANET. Think of TCP/IP as a common language – the computer equivalent of English, which many people around the world speak passably. Using English, an Urdu speaker and a Frenchman could communicate clearly.

TCP/IP was important. Frank Heart of BBN, which built the first IMP for ARPANET, subsequently likened the pre-TCP/IP internet to building a highway then having no cars run on it.

It was born out of a wacky experiment on 22 November 1977, when a grey van drove between San Francisco and San Jose. In the back of the van wasn't a load of parcels but a computer spitting out data that was encoded in the form of radio waves and beamed out into the ether through antennas on the van's roof. Repeaters based in the mountaintops running alongside the stretch of road helped carry the signals to Menlo Park, California, where the radio waves became electrical signals, travelling first across the United States, then across the Atlantic to Goonhilly Earth Station in Cornwall.

There, the signals were pushed into space by satellite dish, bounced off an orbiting satellite, made ground once more at Etam Earth Station in West Virginia and moved back by copper cabling westwards to Marina del Rey, California, just 400 miles from where they started.

The data had criss-crossed the globe and gone through various networks, all in individual packets that could be reconstituted back in California. The interoperability system worked. The test succeeded.

NSFNET was interoperable with ARPANET, but it had one significant difference: it allowed organizations, not just universities, to log on to the internet. Like ARPANET, building it wasn't cheap. One analysis by economists subsequently said government subsidies for NSFNET, as well as for a range of regional networks that ran off it like small tributaries from a major river, cost $160 million. Some $1.6 billion more was likely invested throughout the development of the internet by universities and state governments.

But all that cash had relatively little to show for it. As the world entered the second half of the 1980s, around 2,000 computers were connected to the internet. Nor was it just in the United States that this happened: by 1989, universities and organizations in more than twenty-five countries were connected to the internet. At that point, internet access had broadened out from university departments and commercial organizations to ordinary people: in 1988, the FidoNET BBS network allowed the general public to connect to the internet by relaying the content of Usenet newsgroups, where people congregated online, onto its network.

Goodbye ARPANET

By 1990, one of the most significant shifts in the history of the internet took place. Since that day in October 1969 when the first message – 'Lo' – was sent from one computer to another, ARPANET had provided the backbone of the internet. But as the 1990s loomed, ARPANET was no longer fit for purpose. It was decommissioned over the course of the first half of 1990, replaced by NSFNET. To mark the end of an era, Vint Cerf wrote ARPANET a poem:

It was the first, and being first, was best,
but now we lay it down to ever rest.
Now pause with me a moment, shed some tears.
For auld lang syne, for love, for years and years
of faithful service, duty done, I weep.
Lay down thy packet, now, O friend, and sleep.

NSFNET, which was due to replace the quasi-military network that was ARPANET, wouldn't last long either. By 1993, the company running NSFNET had decided it wasn't economical to do so anymore: it instead opened up the ability for a panoply of private providers to run their own backbone – which at the time angered some but has helped to create the vast tangle of cables that covers our planet, bringing connectivity to many. Five companies initially had enough resources to be able to step in, with more joining later (consolidation, and the high cost of building that infrastructure, means today it's only expanded to around six companies). By 30 April 1995, NSFNET too was decommissioned.

The open market was in charge. And at this point, it's worth thinking about how the internet itself works.

How the internet works

The 'internet' is a portmanteau, a combination of the words 'interconnected' and 'network'.

Each computer, website, server or device connected to the internet has what's called an IP, or internet protocol address, which locates it. (Each has at least one; some have many.) It's the equivalent of a latitude and longitude, locating where you are on the internet. But IP addresses aren't hugely user-friendly; typing in 212.58.233.254 is much more complicated and much harder to remember than typing bbc.co.uk into your web browser, and the rise of so-called dynamic IP addresses, where your position on the internet can shift regularly, makes pinpointing you to a specific IP more challenging. So, we have a user-friendly layer that sits on top of the internet, called the Domain Name System, or DNS.

The DNS was invented by two researchers at the University of Southern California called Paul Mockapetris and Jon Postel, in 1983. It's a digital equivalent of a phone book and made it easier to keep track of the internet as it grew. That phone book had existed before the arrival of the DNS: in the ARPANET days, those overseeing the network maintained a file called hosts.txt, which contained easily understandable addresses for key points on the network. Each machine connected to the network stored this file locally on their devices, and it had to be kept up to date – typically manually. But updating that file became tricky as the number of users increased. So Mockapetris and Postel proposed the DNS, which translates plain text requests to visit locations on the internet into computer-readable ones.

Today, the DNS is constantly being updated and is a decentralized system, with multiple DNS servers stored around the world interacting with one another, making it easy to do those translations quickly. (Postel would also be behind the introduction of TLDs, or top level domains, such as .com, .co.uk, .edu and so on, which he conceived of in 1986. When he died in 1998 at the age of fifty-five, some involved in the running of the internet worried that it might break because Postel held so many secrets about how it worked in his brain.)

The shift from a single, manually maintained database of domain names to a more automated, distributed version is in microcosm the story of the internet's infrastructure. Keeping this thing going becomes ever more challenging as it grows, though the DNS has managed to survive with surprisingly few issues.

As our interest in the World Wide Web has scaled and expanded into apps, streaming services and cloud-based file hosting, so has the internet's infrastructure. But as we'll learn as we track the development of the web from a free-for-all where homegrown, handmade websites dominated to a vertically integrated interface in the hands of a few large providers, the internet data carried across the cables and connections alluded to above is increasingly headed to just a handful of sites and platforms. (We'll get onto this more later.)

Now, six large technology firms – Netflix, Microsoft, Apple, Amazon, Meta (formerly Facebook) and Alphabet (the parent company of Google) – account for 48 per cent of all internet traffic worldwide, according to an analysis by Sandvine, a company that tracks where the bits and bytes go. That proportion is decreasing, by 9 percentage points in 2022, but still shows just how concentrated large parts of our lives and the data that makes them up is in the hands of a small number of companies.

Is this thing on? Online video

For those dabbling in the early days of the internet, the idea that video could be transmitted instantaneously around the world was something they aspired to – but long into the future. Now, it's a well-entrenched fact: two in every three bits of data transmitted around the internet is video. Netflix and YouTube combined account for around a quarter of that video data. Meanwhile TikTok, despite its enormous growth, is responsible for just over 3.5 per cent of video-based internet traffic.

IPv6

Few people give much thought to the infrastructure behind the internet, but by the late 1990s it was becoming important to overhaul some of the elements that made it work. It was increasingly obvious that growth was happening quickly, and there were concerns that it would eventually outpace the limits of how the internet had initially been designed.

IP addresses have gone through two major eras, though confusingly they're not called 1 and 2. They're called 4 and 6.

IPv4, as it was called for short, used 32-bit addresses (like that string of numbers we saw above with bbc.co.uk) to pinpoint each server and website on the internet. The number of bits involved meant that it was possible to have 4.3 billion unique IP addresses online. That may seem like enough, but there was a recognition – and a worry by the 1990s – that what seemed like endless space online might actually end up running out. Efficiently running the system was also a major contributing factor to overhauling the tech.

So the Internet Engineering Task Force, a group that oversaw standards on the internet, set to work developing a new version of IP addresses. IPv6 was first released in 1998, changing the 32-bit address system into a much larger 128-bit one. However, IPv4 still remains dominant, for a number of reasons. While we're still largely using IPv4, the upgrade to IPv6 meant that in theory the maximum capacity of the IP database went from 4.3 billion entries to 340 trillion trillion trillion (no, that isn't a typo). The internet wouldn't run out of addresses, and we could all enjoy its benefits.

Undersea cables

For a world-changing, cutting-edge technology, the infrastructure behind the internet can seem quite old-fashioned. A significant proportion of the data that worms its way into your mind through your devices each day is transported through undersea cables that criss-cross the Earth.

In all, there are 529 cable systems that sit on the ocean floors, transmitting data daily around the world. Dozens link the UK to Europe, the United States and Canada alone, run by large internet infrastructure companies. And if something goes wrong with them, as can occasionally happen if a volcano erupts, a fishing vessel drags its anchor over them, or if there's a deliberate incident of sabotage, it can be expensive to fix – millions of dollars at a time. Keeping those cables working isn't cheap, and nor is ensuring new connections keep the world in touch online. Spending on new system infrastructure topped $2.7 billion in 2020, through a number of private–public partnerships.

The biggest new cable, the 2Africa connection, which will span 45,000 kilometres between Africa, Europe and Asia, linked in Europe to the Port of Marseille, is an engineering wonder. The 2Africa cable, which encircles Africa with spurs off to Europe and Asia and the Middle East, is longer than the circumference of the Earth and will connect thirty-three countries more quickly to the

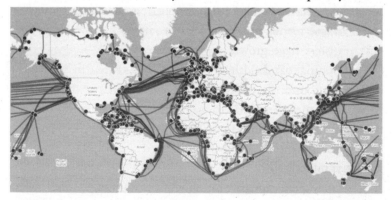

A map of all the submarine communications cables around the world, as of July 2015.

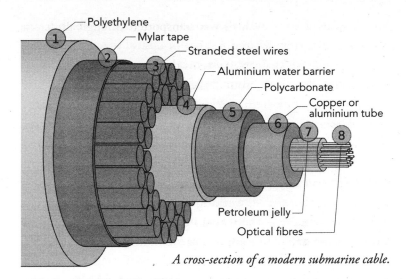

Polyethylene
Mylar tape
Stranded steel wires
Aluminium water barrier
Polycarbonate
Copper or aluminium tube
Petroleum jelly
Optical fibres

A cross-section of a modern submarine cable.

internet when it's completed in 2024. The cabling can carry 180 terabits of data a second, equivalent to downloading 7,500 high-definition movies from Netflix in an instant. The consortium overseeing the project is led by social media company Meta but includes a range of internet service providers (ISPs), including Vodafone, Orange and China Mobile. (One corollary of the rise of social media and Big Tech means that the demands for data transfers have grown, and so those companies responsible for ballooning bandwidth often have to foot the bill to fund its infrastructure. So-called content providers such as Google, Facebook, Amazon and Microsoft lease or own more than half the world's subsea bandwidth.)

It's a costly enterprise. Overall, the 2Africa project is expected to cost $1 billion.

That may seem expensive for something that's around an inch in diameter, similar to the size of a regular garden hose (and possible to confuse for that, too). But they're a marvel of engineering: an outer layer of plastic shrouds a web of copper tubing, which covers steel wires that wrap around a range of optical fibres – thin glass tubes through which light passes, carrying data along the way. These cables can run for miles, from one landmass to another.

Not that it's uninterrupted. Impurities within the fibre-optic cable at the core of internet links stop light travelling forever, meaning that every so often it needs to be boosted by repeaters. These stops tend to be every 50 miles or so (the 730 repeaters that are part of the 2Africa cable pop up every 61 kilometres, or 38 miles) and take the fibre connection and amplify it, sending it back on its journey. Without that boosting, bits of data would go missing as the signal drops in strength.

Once the data signals arrive on shore, their transcontinental, underwater journey complete, they're then passed on to onshore cables that traverse the country. The cables within a country are very similar to those that lie deep underwater, but they come with a complication: it's difficult to figure out where to put them. Space on land is often limited, and so companies laying large cables across a country often choose to try to place them alongside existing infrastructure, such as gas pipelines or electricity cables. A surprising number sit alongside major roads or rail lines – because these provide already existing, simple and uninterrupted paths for key bits of infrastructure to sit safely.

As those large fibre-optic cables reach key cities, they will often branch out in different directions. Some households have what's called 'fibre to the home', which continues the fibre-optic cabling – albeit at a smaller scale – direct to a person's property. This type of internet connection is superfast because it maintains the high speeds possible through fibre cabling (though some ISPs cheat and use copper cabling within their own systems). A second, more common connection is called 'fibre to the cabinet'.

Here, the fibre-optic cables lead to a telephone cabinet near to a neighbourhood of houses, at which point the internet signal hops from fibre-optic to copper cabling, similar to the older ways of connecting to the internet more popular in the 1990s and 2000s, to get to your home.

How do you connect?

Today, most people never have to 'connect' to the internet. Almost all internet connections are now always-on, pretty fast, broadband connections – though that is a comparatively recent development when looking at the long history of the internet. There was a time when you had to connect and endure a crackly dial tone and screeching series of tones as your computer linked up to the internet through your phone line. If you're of a certain age, you're welcome for being hit with that wave of nostalgia. If you're too young to know what we're talking about … ask your parents.

That connection was made through a modem, built in to your computer. Modems are bits of computer hardware that translate or modulate the digital, binary signals produced by data (0 or 1, depending on whether it's off or on) into analogue, tonal signals that can be sent down phone lines. The word 'modem' is a word created by shoving two other words together: 'modulator-demodulator', which is what the tool does.

Modems have existed since the 1920s and were used in the Second World War and Cold War eras to speedily transmit radar images from one location to another. At that time, they weren't connected to computers but were entirely analogue. But whether digital or analogue, a modem works the same: they modulate computer-based signals into phone-based signals, then demodulate the phone signals back into computer-readable signals when they arrive at the destination computer.

*An example of
an early acoustic
coupler modem.*

That use of a modem to transmit data for military purposes, like much of the internet, became something that was then expanded to suit more general use. The first commercial modem, the Bell 103, was released in the 1960s. It acted as a cradle onto which a phone's handset was placed, so that the sound signals that came through the receiver could seamlessly be picked up by the modem. Those modems could be used to connect to early bulletin boards, transmitting the data that kept people in touch through the BBSes. Early modems weren't quick; they started at around 110 bits per second (bps) before moving up to 300bps. For comparison, the modems used in the early peak of the internet were 56,000bps.

The bulletin board became a staple form of communication in the early days of the internet, predating the World Wide Web. And it was created in part because of a blizzard that killed hundreds of people.

The Great Blizzard struck the Great Lakes, Ohio Valley and southern Ontario in late January 1978. It brought Chicago to a halt, meaning that an IBM programmer named Ward Christensen couldn't get to work. IBM was at the time a technology monolith, the equivalent of Microsoft or Apple today. Instead of going to work, Christensen decided to devote his time to a project he had conceived of that would help build a kind of digital noticeboard, where users could leave messages for others who would log on later.

The new invention was called a Computerized Bulletin Board System, or CBBS, which was later shortened to BBS. It would mark the first home for the concept of the online community that would dictate and sway public discussion on the internet – the forebear of the fandoms that we will learn about in Chapter 5.

In the early days, when the internet wasn't widely accessible or well known, modems were third-party peripherals that you could buy and plug into your PC. The first PC modem was created in 1977 by Dale Heatherington and Dennis Hayes; the 80-103A launched their business into success, as well as establishing an industry of modems. But as the price of producing them dropped and uptake of the internet rose, they began to be built in to PCs from the mid-1980s as IBM personal computers started to spread into homes and businesses. It took until the 1990s for the price to drop to such an extent that it became basically impossible to buy a computer without an integrated modem, helped somewhat by the development of the Winmodem, a bit of software that outsourced some of the work required from a modem from the hardware, making it cheaper to produce.

Of course, today few people solely connect to the internet through a desktop computer or laptop. We don't have to plug ourselves into the wall and proactively connect to the internet by dialling a phone number connected to an ISP and transmitting our username and password through the screeches and hisses enabled through a modem. Instead, as you know, the internet is always on and accessible to a panoply of devices through a router. The router is a box that brokers connections between your devices and the wider internet, and often has Wi-Fi, which was first conceived of in the early 1990s and was released to the world, under the guise of 'wireless networking', in September 1997.

CompuServe is born

But let's wind back a bit. The hardware pre-dated the companies that helped broker those connections by quite a long way. It took until 1979 for CompuServe, then launched as MicroNET in Radio Shack stores for those buying the retailer's comparatively accessible Tandy Model 100 computers, to appear on the internet. CompuServe is widely regarded as one of the first customer-facing, dial-up online information services, though it had started in 1969 as a timesharing service for businesses looking to access computers to do their accounts.

In the late 1970s and 1980s, CompuServe became popular because of its online chat service, the CB Simulator (so named because it mimicked citizen band, or CB, radio).

By 1989, CompuServe offered ordinary internet users the opportunity to email other people outside CompuServe, as well as a massive range of lively discussion forums to participate in. It was joined by Prodigy, a competing service, which launched in September 1990. Where CompuServe was text-only, Prodigy offered users the ability to interact through basic graphical interfaces, which included rudimentary pictures and buttons alongside the walls of text that typified the early internet.

Both would become some of the main gateways to the internet in the 1980s and 1990s with their custom-curated, gated communities of users. (Prodigy would be the first to allow users to browse the wider web in December 1994.) But they would also be supplanted in time by a nimbler competitor that popularized the internet, and later the web, called AOL – but we'll learn about that later.

What happens on the World Wide Web?

As we've explored, the transfer of data through the internet long pre-dated the World Wide Web. While most of us now think of visiting websites through the internet as if it's magic, typing in a URL (uniform resource locator, such as www.google.com) and finding ourselves on the website we want, things behind the scenes are much more complicated.

What's involved in every step you make on the web is a series of call and responses – a giant game of Marco Polo. From your internet protocol (IP) address, your computer, phone or tablet will send out a signal. It's a request to visit a specific website. The website, after receiving your request, will then send back information allowing you to visit it. Your request will often be routed through a number of different IP points as it tries to find the quickest route possible to its destination.

When that connection is made and assured, the server hosting the information you're seeking – whether it's a rail company's website to buy a ticket or a hotel's website on which you're trying to view the picture of the pool – will then start sending you the content, packet by packet.

It's a similar series of events that have always happened on the internet, right back to the earliest days of our online lives when researchers at one university would connect digitally with those at another institution and directly transfer files from one computer to another. But if you think that every hotel, from the big chains to the smallest, family-run bed and breakfast, has their own server running behind their website ready to deliver you the data needed to access their website, think again.

If every website were to host their data at source, it would mean that browsing the internet could take forever, as your request tried to cross the world, attempting to find a route to retrieve the data. Instead, what happens in some instances is that the data is distributed, with 'local' copies stored by businesses called content delivery networks, or CDNs. These CDNs will store copies of what it thinks will be popular among web users – for instance, copies of the latest trendy Netflix series – and will store it at multiple locations around the world.

The theory is that when you want to watch it one evening, your laptop or internet-connected smart TV doesn't have to travel halfway around the planet in order to seek out a version. It can look closer to home. The same principle happens in the offline world: supermarkets stock toilet roll locally in their back rooms for ease of access by shoppers, rather than waiting until you need it and asking the factory to send some over.

If you're lucky, and the website or streaming video or audio you're seeking is popular, you'll find a local version. But if it's rarer, the connection request your device put out on your behalf might have further to travel to find a version. Occasionally, it'll have to cross oceans.

All this happens unnoticed in an instant. The difference in time between you asking to visit a website that's stored at a data centre nearby and one stored in a different country is a fraction of a second. If, like me, you live just outside a city 300 miles from London, it can take 2 to 5 milliseconds – or 2 to 5 one-thousandths of a second – to find a popular website stored in a data centre in the middle of the city. If it's not there and your request has to travel down to London, it can take another 20 milliseconds. If it still can't be found, and your data request has to cross the Atlantic to New York to find the closest copy, you can add another 80 or so milliseconds. Rarely, the data might not be held at a data centre on the eastern seaboard of the United States, in which case your request might have to travel all the way to San Francisco – which adds another 80 milliseconds.

Once the required file is found, whether it's a video, a web page or an individual element of it like a picture, it then has to travel back the same route, which takes the same amount of time again. Each step is retraced carefully. But it gets a bit more complicated: files don't travel as a whole. Instead, they're chopped up into packets, or small sections. Each of those packets travels separately back to your device, where they're then reassembled. It's like breaking up a file or web page into pieces like a jigsaw, then putting them back together when they arrive at their destination.

How the web is secured: Heartbleed

In 2014, decades after the internet was invented, and more than twenty years after it was commercialized, the world began to realise quite how reliant our digital lives were on the goodwill of hobbyists volunteering their time. That March, researchers at Google discovered a vulnerability that would later be dubbed Heartbleed.

It was a single, small problem in the 456,332 lines of code that made up OpenSSL, a volunteer-led organization that maintained a popular implementation of the TLS, or transport layer security protocol. In short, OpenSSL was an encrypted security toolkit – a quick, easy and free way for sites as varied as Gmail, Netflix and Etsy to keep the transportation of our data secure.

But those Big Tech organizations were leveraging the goodwill of a handful of overworked volunteers – who ended up making mistakes. When a computer pings a server using OpenSSL, it asks both sides to provide a 'heartbeat' – a tiny packet of data to prove both parties are working correctly. But a coding error meant that anyone who wanted to could ask a server to return a heartbeat larger than expected: up to 64k of memory, or enough text to repeat the Gettysburg address forty-four times.

Heartbleed meant that websites were spilling data they weren't meant to. Every time they were pinged they could vomit out 64k of information. Sometimes that was innocuous. Other times it included passwords or personal details. And an estimated two-thirds of the world's websites used OpenSSL. This was a problem. And it was left to two men named Steve – Steve Marquess and Stephen Henson, who oversaw much of the OpenSSL code base – to fix. After plenty of long nights and a good deal of stress, an update to the OpenSSL code was quickly drawn up and the problem fixed.

Realizing quite how important the work of those volunteers was, Big Tech companies started funding the OpenSSL Foundation, which was overseeing the security of us all. It was a reminder of how much of our digital experience is cobbled together – the collective cruft of decades of history.

How the web came to be

By the late 1980s, internet access had moved from elite universities to a broader range of institutions – but still largely remained the preserve of those who were looking to communicate with fellow researchers or to chat with each other on bulletin boards and newsgroups.

To take the internet from the domain of the tech-literate to the everyday user, it needed a simple-to-use interface. That came about with the arrival of the World Wide Web, the invention of Tim Berners-Lee.

In 1989, Berners-Lee, a British researcher, was working at CERN, a Switzerland-based nuclear research laboratory that would later become famous for housing the Large Hadron Collider. The researcher saw the potential of the internet beyond the small, largely academic community that inhabited it at the time. But

Tim Berners-Lee, in a photograph from 1996.

more pressingly, he felt there was a way to make communication between fellow researchers better, and so set about building what he called at its christening the World Wide Web.

In March 1989, Berners-Lee submitted a proposal for what he described as 'information management'. The document outlined the problems of loss of information among researchers, particularly how the complex, ever-evolving systems they utilized worked as they evolved rapidly. That proposal, and a second one tabled in May 1990, proposed a solution to the issue that blighted CERN: 'How will we ever keep track of such a large project?'

The answer? The judicious use of hypertext.

Hypertext was something Berners-Lee was very familiar with. He had written a program in 1980 to keep track of software he was involved in developing called Enquire. 'To find information, one progressed via the links from one sheet to another, rather like in the old computer game "Adventure",' Berners-Lee wrote in his 1990 proposal. Those links – at the time a foreign concept – were displayed using hypertext, a term coined decades earlier by a filmmaker-turned-computer programmer called Ted Nelson.

Berners-Lee described hypertext as defined by Nelson as 'human-readable information linked together in an unconstrained way'. Essentially, you could leap from one concept to another, using the links Berners-Lee had developed as part of his Enquire program.

He managed to convince some colleagues in CERN about the utility of his idea, including Belgian systems engineer Robert Cailliau. With Cailliau, Berners-Lee wrote to CERN management with a more formal proposal in November 1990. That proposal was notable not only because it marked a real moment in the history of the internet but because the terminology it used to describe concepts is still in common use today:

> HyperText is a way to link and access information of various kinds as a web of nodes in which the user can browse at will. It provides a single user-interface to large classes of information (reports, notes, data-bases, computer documentation and on-line help). We propose a simple scheme incorporating servers already available at CERN.

The duo asked CERN for four software engineers, a programmer and computers for all those accessing the new system, which he said should be called the World Wide Web.

The project was given the go-ahead, and Berners-Lee had

the first ever web server installed at CERN as 1990 turned into 1991. The computer needed to remain permanently online, so he put a note on it in red ink: 'This machine is a server. DO NOT POWER IT DOWN!!'

The first ever website was one of Berners-Lee's own making, hosted on CERN's server. It included information about what the World Wide Web project was, and how it worked.

Giving the web the hard sell

The 1991 ACM Hypertext conference was held in San Antonio, Texas. Berners-Lee was there with his World Wide Web concept, but conference-goers were dubious. 'There was nothing very clever about the system,' Professor Wendy Hall, a contemporary of Berners-Lee later recalled thinking. Hall thought the name was pretentious, and she wasn't alone in her scepticism: the paper proposing the World Wide Web was rejected from the conference. Still, Berners-Lee hung around the sidelines, demonstrating his concept.

At least one person there thought it was interesting – the first web server outside CERN came online in the United States at Stanford University's particle physics laboratory. However, accessing websites was clunky. You could use a more fully featured browser if you had a NeXT computer, a specific type of computer aimed at the educational market that cost the equivalent of around $16,100 today. But, for those who couldn't afford that or couldn't access a NeXT computer through their university, there was a 'line mode' web browser, which was very user-unfriendly. An alternative was needed.

Mosaic: the first popular web browser

By December 1992, programmers Marc Andreessen and Eric Bina had realized that the web's promise would never live up to its potential if there wasn't an easy, intuitive browser through which to navigate the World Wide Web.

Andreessen and Bina worked at the National Center for Supercomputing Applications (NCSA), which was based at the University of Illinois. They used funding provided to the NCSA by the 1991 High Performance Computing Act, which was developed and passed by future vice-president Al Gore, to design a web browser. (Gore is often mocked, unfairly, for claiming to be involved in the invention of the internet, but without what was called informally the 'Gore Act', it's unlikely the internet would have become quite as widespread quite as quickly.)

Their browser, released as a beta version on 23 January 1993, was called Mosaic. Andreessen published the program to the internet with a message saying, 'By the power vested in me by nobody in particular, alpha/beta version 0.5 of ... X Mosaic is hereby released.'

The mocking hyperbole belied the impact Mosaic had. It helped bring the web to the masses. Mosaic was simple to use, and available on Macintosh and Windows computers – which were rapidly coming down in price. It also showcased the qualities of the web to an audience that would become its most ardent adherents – unlike competing early browsers around at the time, Mosaic would display images right alongside text, showing off the multimedia qualities of the web.

By the end of 1993, the browser and its creators were being profiled by *The New York Times*. By this point, more than 5,000 people every month were downloading Mosaic – astronomical figures at the time, given there were only 500 or so known web servers. Mosaic was listed as one of *Fortune* magazine's

A screenshot of the Mosaic web browser.

products of the year in 1994, in the good company of the Mighty Morphin Power Rangers and the Wonderbra. *WIRED*, the in-house magazine for the booming tech sector, also sung Mosaic's praises:

> Mosaic's charming appearance encourages users to load their own documents onto the Net, including color photos, sound bites, video clips, and hypertext 'links' to other documents. By following the links – click, and the linked document appears – you can travel through the online world along paths of whim and intuition.

The title of that *WIRED* article? 'The (Second Phase of the) Revolution Has Begun'. The web era was upon us.

1994: the year of the web

As calendars flicked from 1993 to 1994, the web was still comparatively small. But it wouldn't stay small for long.

The groundwork for its growth had been laid by a piece of legislation that passed through the US Congress on 26 July 1993. The National Information Infrastructure Act included an impetus for the weight of government to make the internet as widely accessible to as many people as possible, as quickly as possible. It meant that the internet, and the web, had big backing.

In 1994, two blockbuster conferences took place – one at CERN in Geneva, and one in the United States. The Geneva claque, called the First International Conference on the World-Wide Web, took place between 25 and 27 May 1994, and saw 380 people attend. Those there called it the 'Woodstock of the web'. The United States conference was larger – by dint, perhaps, of the concentration of web-literate computer scientists in the States – hosting 1,300 people at the International WWW Conference in October.

Those 500 known web servers at the end of 1993 became 10,000 by the end of 1994. Some 10 million people logged on to the web. CERN itself tracked that the level of web traffic was the equivalent of sending the entire collected works of William Shakespeare – every single second.

The rapid growth of the web was exciting, but those behind its invention recognized that there needed to be some order. Berners-Lee left CERN to join the Massachusetts Institute of Technology, where he founded the International World Wide Web Consortium (W3C), a standards-setting body. The principle behind W3C was to establish key baselines for the web, but it was also an attempt by

Berners-Lee to ensure that the web would remain open to all. The consortium was established to protect its future.

While the bureaucrats behind W3C were keen to make sure the web worked for everyone, individuals were keen to plant their own flags on this new territory and build their own personal homes there. At the same time, quick-thinking businesspeople were all too aware of the money-making potential of being first movers in what we now call Web 1.0. In February 1994, author Dave Taylor set about writing a magazine article on the number of companies carrying out business online. He was surprised to learn there was no centralized database – so he set about making his own, called 'The Internet Mall'. It started with thirty-four companies but would quickly grow.

As would the web itself. If the 1960s and '70s were the military's era of the internet, and the 1980s focus migrated to government control of academia, the 1990s saw the full force of capitalism, competition and privatization hit.

Chapter 2
Web 1.0

Welcome to AOL

The web really came into its own thanks to competition among ISPs and out-of-the-box thinking from one in particular: AOL.

The company was born in the pre-web era, back in 1988. Quantum Computer Services was running a dial-up online service for Commodore 64 users, called QuantumLink. Quantum helped create a similar product, at a cost of $5 million, for Apple computers called AppleLink – though the business relationship quickly became strained as Apple demanded exacting rules from Quantum.

A year later, Quantum took the failed AppleLink project and generalized it away from one specific set of computers. They called their new product America Online. AOL was a walled garden that offered instant messaging, chat rooms and online gaming – alongside a series of channels which acted as gateways to online communities around shared interests. AOL released a version of its software for MS-DOS (Microsoft Disk Operating System) in 1991, and by 1992 AOL had more than 150,000 subscribers. AOL went public that same year, raising $66 million.

But AOL was still lagging behind competitors like CompuServe and Prodigy. It was easier to use than both, with a simple installation process and a user-friendly interface, typified by the welcoming voice of Washington DC broadcaster Elwood Edwards, who was paid $100 to be the voice of the service as he greeted those logging on with the words 'Welcome to AOL' and 'You've got mail', if they were lucky. But actually getting people to use it proved tricky.

The floppy disk fable

Jan Brandt had the answer. She became AOL's vice-president of marketing in 1993 and asked for a budget of $250,000 to produce 200,000 floppy disks with AOL pre-installed that would be given out for free. Once people saw AOL, she reckoned, they would sign up.

Brandt's hunch was correct. One in ten of those who got a disk then signed up – vast numbers for a marketing campaign. Floppy disks became CDs; at one point half of all CDs produced worldwide were emblazoned with AOL's logo.

AOL had a million users by August 1994. By February 1995, it was 2 million. By May 1996, it was 5 million, at which point CompuServe and Prodigy had been left in the dust. Half of the internet-connected population in the US used AOL by 1997. The rise of the internet is commensurate with the rise of home computers – because without a way to get online, there's no reason to have an internet connection. The proportion of homes that had computers began to rise over time, but in the early days of the World Wide Web the number was still small. In 1992, only 23 per cent of American households had a computer.

And just because they had a computer didn't mean they had the internet. Many people didn't see the need: by 1995, only 14 per cent of Americans used the internet. Even by 2000, at the height of the dot-com boom, a minority of Americans were online: 46 per cent.

Many of those that were, however, were on AOL. And somehow the company still persists even today, decades after dial-up connections disappeared. Around 1.5 million people still give the company $9.99 or $14.99 a month for technical support and identity theft protection – likely a hangover from their 1990s internet connection deals they never cancelled.

The spreading popularity of the web and the wider internet took many of those who had long made it their home by surprise. Starting in September 1993, those longer-tenured internet denizens began to notice an influx of new users, many of whom disrupted the old norms and ignored the unwritten rules of how to behave online.

The new users were brought online by an agreement between Usenet and a number of ISPs to allow free access to the former; AOL was a major contributor, developing a Usenet gateway service in March 1994. It echoed the demographic shifts that had occurred every September previously on the internet, when new students arrived at their university and gained access to the internet through on-campus computer clusters – and needed gentle coaxing into learning the rules of the road on the information superhighway (a phrase we can also attribute to Al Gore).

The problem was that with the normal academic onrush of students, things got back to normal within a few weeks as people settled down, used the network less and adopted the habits of experienced users. With AOL, that never happened – the problem was persistent and year-round. Which is how the phenomenon gained the name 'Eternal September'.

Those joining the internet in that Eternal September weren't just rank-and-file users. While Queen Elizabeth II may have been in on the email game early, it took until 4 February 1994 for the first email exchange between two world leaders. Carl Bildt, then Sweden's prime minister, sent an email to Bill Clinton, then the US president, congratulating him on ending a trade embargo levied against Vietnam. Clinton replied thanking Bildt for his words and sharing excitement about the internet. Twenty-five years later, Bildt posted a picture of printouts of the emails to – where else? – Twitter. 'Now literally a museum piece,' he wrote.

My home page

The web quickly became a home away from home for those early adopters who were keen to make their presence felt. They realized they could put the linking qualities of hypertext to good use to create their own homesteads online. The personal web page flourished.

This changed the web, which had previously been a staid, bookish place where university lecturers – most of them in physics or other science subjects – would dump their lecture notes for students to peruse outside of class. That shift away from university labs towards a more open, democratic, representative web was enabled by a raft of different companies who offered free hosting on the internet using their own servers, including companies whose names are now lost to many younger internet users' minds, like GeoCities.

GeoCities – or as it was then called, Beverly Hills Internet – was formed in November 1994 by David Bohnett and John Rezner. The two entrepreneurs ran one of the earliest web hosting and development companies online, offering to design and maintain websites for companies who sought to be early adopters of the web.

What would later become GeoCities in 1995 was a way for the Beverly Hills Internet Co. to market its wares. The idea was that you would come to the site to get your free plot of land in the new digital world – GeoCities offered users a whopping 2 megabytes of storage onto which they could build and store their own personal website – and then migrate over to its paid-for services.

GeoCities users were literally called 'homesteaders', evoking the idea that these were new settlers establishing a life for themselves in a strange new territory. And those homesteaders grew in number as an ever-increasing proportion of users decided they didn't want to just browse the web, they wanted to plant their own flag upon it. By the end of 1995, thousands of new users were signing up every day; sites hosted on GeoCities received more than 6 million page views every single month.

It kept growing, despite competition from other services like Tripod and Angelfire, which also offered free hosting and storage for your website. By October 1997, GeoCities was the fifth most popular website on the whole World Wide Web and had a million users hosting their own home pages through the site. GeoCities launched on the stock market in August 1998 and was bought by Yahoo for $3.57 billion in January 1999. (It would end up closing in 2009, as the make-up of the web changed and people stopped creating personal websites, reasoning that their social media profiles were now their own little corner of the internet.)

But between the personal website and the social media era, there was an interregnum: blogging.

The rise of blogging

One of the key elements that exemplified the early web was the ability to express yourself online. But early home pages, including those hosted on GeoCities, didn't fully capture the idea of an online diary – or weblog, which would later be shortened to blog. In the 1990s, those early blogs – pithy updates, shared with the rest of the web – required web pages to be manually updated.

Blog all about it!

The impact of blogging is hard to overstate. It shifted how we analyze and understand the world, with massive ramifications for how journalism now works in the digital space. Instead of relying on perfectly packaged summaries the morning after an event happens, we now expect to be able to view a live blog, pithily capturing events as they occur.

The first inkling of this new journalism/blogging hybrid being the future came in 1998, when a former sales executive working in the CBS studios gift shop ran a story on his blog – The Drudge Report – that no other news organization would: then US president Bill Clinton was rumoured to have had a sexual dalliance with an aide in the Oval Office. Drudge's willingness to publish and be damned nearly spelled the end of Clinton's career – and it showed the value of blogging.

Still, people did it. The phrase 'weblog' was coined by Jorn Barger, the owner of a website named Robot Wisdom, who called a collection of links he had encountered and recommended to others on his site a weblog in December 1997. Around the same time, a techblog called Slashdot launched, and shortly afterwards, in March 1999, Brad Fitzpatrick (one of the earliest web bloggers) developed a blogging platform he called LiveJournal. Soon, millions of users were updating their LiveJournals, including teenagers who swapped out their secret paper diaries for public-facing internet facsimiles.

But it was Blogger, the brainchild of Ev Williams, who would later go on to play a role in the creation of Twitter, that really kick-started blogging online. Launched in August 1999, Blogger had a reputation as more of a grown-up platform for blogging, encouraging people to think of blogs as a halfway house between the diaries they had started off as and the journalism they sought to ape. Blogger was bought by Google in 2003 and remains active today but has been overtaken by content management systems like Wordpress.

Netscape Navigator

With the number of websites ballooning in the mid-1990s, finding your way around the web was more important than ever. As we learned in the last chapter, Mosaic helped usher in the web era, but it would undergo a transformation in October 1994.

The University of Illinois, where Mosaic had been developed, were wary of Andreessen and Bina commercializing their product. But both the developers saw the potential of being the main method of browsing the nascent web, so they sought to go it alone. Mosaic was rebranded Navigator, a product of the company Netscape Communications, and spun out of the university.

Navigator was a boon for early browsers of the World Wide Web. Unlike its predecessors, which waited until all the elements of a web page were downloaded before displaying it to users, Navigator did it on the fly. At a time when internet connections were often agonizingly slow, that was a useful tool, allowing people to scroll through the quicker-to-load text content on a website while they waited for images and other multimedia content to display. It also contained a new innovation: cookies. These little nuggets of data would remember where you were logged in on websites so you didn't have to keep entering usernames and passwords, but they would eventually become a helpful tool for advertisers looking to track users as they browsed.

By 1995, Netscape had a 40 per cent share of the browser market, and had nearly doubled that by 1996. That was a big deal: there were 45 million people on the internet that year – an increase of 76 per cent from the year before. (That level of growth was nothing compared to the leap in the number of websites, which grew nearly 1,000 per cent in the same time period.) As it turned out, 1995 would be Netscape's apogee, as a war was beginning over who would control the method of helping us travel through the World Wide Web. Netscape launched its IPO on 9 August 1995, floating at an initial price of $14 a share.

The markets opened that morning, but Netscape wasn't available to buy. Far from being a worry, it was a blessing for Andreessen and his company. Buyers were so keen to get stock in the company that the market couldn't be arranged in an orderly fashion. It took ninety minutes to sort out, by which point retail investment company Charles Schwab had set up a special recording for concerned customers calling them, telling them to press 1 if they were interested in investing in Netscape. By 11 a.m., the first trades in Netscape took place at $71. They'd peak that day at $75. The *Wall Street Journal* wrote: 'It took General Dynamics Corp. forty-three years to become a corporation worth $2.7 billion. It took Netscape Communications Corp. about a minute.'

Microsoft, which was quickly becoming a major force in the tech space, was watching on. And it wanted in.

Internet Explorer

Microsoft began to realize the power that the internet would have as it saw people downloading, then using, Navigator's predecessor Mosaic to surf the net. So, they decided to get in on the act. In the summer of 1994, they put employee Thomas Reardon to work tinkering with the source code of a commercial version of Mosaic they had bought from a company called Spyglass, which handled the rights to the browser.

The Mosaic that Microsoft bought access to wasn't the same one as produced by the academic team at the NCSA, but it shared its underlying features. The development team at Spyglass had built their own version from scratch, which looked and acted like the original Mosaic. Microsoft inherited that and set to work developing its own web browser.

Building this browser was a pressing, prime concern for Microsoft, and one that the company's chief executive, Bill Gates, saw as integral to its future survival. Initially, Gates was said to have been blasé about the rise of the internet, reasoning that his operating system was on practically every PC sold across the world – enough control for him over the market.

But by late May 1995, he had changed his mind. In a memo to employees titled 'The Internet Tidal Wave', Gates explained that simply squatting in its dominant position wouldn't be enough:

In the next twenty years the improvement in computer power will be outpaced by the exponential improvements in communications networks … A combination of expanded access to the Internet, ISDN, new broadband networks justified by video based applications and interconnections between each of these will bring low cost communication to most businesses and homes within the next decade.

The Internet is at the forefront of all of this and developments on the Internet over the next several years will set the course of our industry for a long time to come. Perhaps you have already seen memos from me or others here about the importance of the Internet. I have gone through several stages of increasing my views of its importance. Now I assign the Internet the highest level of importance. In this memo I want to make clear that our focus on the Internet is crucial to every part of our business.

The Internet is the most important single development to come along since the IBM PC was introduced in 1981. It is even more important than the arrival of the graphical user interface.

Gates outlined five priorities for Microsoft to work on to take advantage of this significant shift. One of them was work on the 'client' – the tool that would compete with Netscape Navigator, which at that time had a 70 per cent market share.

Microsoft threw more staff and resources into what would become the company's billboard browser. Reardon was joined by a handful of other Microsoft employees to turn Spyglass Mosaic into Internet Explorer. Version one of the web browser was released in August 1995, as part of the Windows 95 operating system which became the standard for many PCs sold to users.

The browser wars begin

Soon Microsoft began bundling Internet Explorer into its operating system, and it allowed people to download version two of the program from the internet in November 1995. Free access to Internet Explorer was a significant step away from the likes of Netscape Navigator, which asked its users to pay to use it. This would soon change, however, as it also became free to use.

But slashing the price of Navigator to nothing couldn't arrest Internet Explorer's rise – at Netscape's expense. Internet Explorer 3.0, released in 1996, was widely seen as a match for Netscape's browser, and Microsoft quickly passed 10 per cent share of the browser market that year. By 1998, around four in every ten web users found their way around the internet using Microsoft's tool. By 2000, it was double that number. They were browsing

17 million websites, compared to a few tens of thousands when Internet Explorer was first released.

Netscape was wiped out; Microsoft became dominant. But something didn't sit right.

Microsoft gained its position at the top of the totem pole through anti-competitive practices, alleged Netscape in a complaint made

---

Secondary skirmishes

Internet Explorer was largely a Windows tool, but Apple users still needed a web browser. Safari, developed by the Cupertino company in 2003, was their alternative. But it was a phoenix rising from the ashes of Netscape's failure that would prove the toughest challenge for Internet Explorer as the mid-2000s arrived.

Mozilla Firefox was built largely off the back of Netscape Navigator, but it removed some of the extraneous features that its developers believed Netscape had included to try to appease its commercial sponsors. That pared back design also helped Mozilla present a point of difference to Internet Explorer, which was dominant but stagnant and facing middle-aged spread. Initially called Phoenix as a deliberate attempt to pick up on the imagery of rising from Navigator's ashes, it was renamed twice due to trademark claims: first to Firebird, then to Firefox.

It was released in November 2004 and quickly became popular, gaining 60 million downloads in its first nine months of existence. At its height five years later, it had one third of the browser market, but it would soon be overtaken by yet another browser: one developed by Google.

---

to the US federal government in May 1998. The courts agreed. In April 2000, in his decision in the *United States* v. *Microsoft Corp.* case, Judge Thomas Jackson decreed Microsoft was guilty of monopolization.

By then, though, there was little stopping Internet Explorer. Microsoft's browser ended up with 95 per cent market share by the early 2000s – though competitors would soon be coming around the corner.

Chrome-plated

Google had built its business by being invaluable to internet users. People used its free webmail service, Gmail, and regularly visited its search engine to discover new corners of the web. They kept their diaries on Google Calendar, launched in 2006, and would later use Google's web-based productivity software. There were few areas Google didn't touch.

Except the browser. In September 2008, wanting to cement its central position in people's digital lives, Google unveiled Chrome, a web browser it had built in secret. Chrome was quick, easy to use and integrated all of Google's tools innately into the browser experience. It replicated Microsoft's model of making a smooth user experience as much as possible.

Google, perhaps seeing the issues that Microsoft had gotten into over Internet Explorer's dominance in the 1990s, was at pains to say it didn't imagine that it could supplant Firefox or Internet Explorer with Chrome – though that lie didn't last long. By 2013, Chrome was the world's most widely used web browser, and it has retained that position to this day.

Exploring the boundaries of the web

Much as many people go out for a joy ride when they buy their first car, to enjoy their new-found freedom, so too users would explore their chosen web browsers once they had installed them and got the hang of them, to discover all the things the web could offer.

That would include stopping in on the personal websites of their friends alongside some of the early established sites, including popular websites like Ask Jeeves, which launched in June 1996 and presented its answer engine (as opposed to search engine) technology in the form of an anthropomorphized English butler called Jeeves, who would deliver the answers to your questions.

The most popular website in the early 1990s was AOL.com – by dint of the fact that most people used AOL as their ISP and so would automatically be taken there. But scouting around the web could unveil other treasures hidden in plain sight, such as Cybergrass, which was initially hosted on the Palo Alto Research Center's servers when launched in September 1992 and was the first music site on the internet (devoted to bluegrass music). Or the Internet Movie Database, better known today as IMDb, which piggybacked on Cardiff University's computer science department's servers and hosted movie reviews.

Those really wanting to test their new internet connections might find their way to a web page hosted by Cambridge University called the Trojan Room Coffee Machine. There, they could watch a grainy, flickering live feed of a coffee pot in the university's computer laboratory. The website went live on the web in 1993 but had existed on Cambridge University's private network for the previous two years. The website – the world's first webcam – acted as a diversion for browsers in the early days of the internet, but it was a utility for those working in the computer science department: they could simply check the image to see if there was fresh coffee to pour without leaving their desks.

Just chatting

Those early websites were generally what computer scientists like those watching the coffee-pot camera would call 'read only': you passively consumed the content upon them, rather than interacting with it or each other. In some ways, the early web was a step back from the raucous, interactive internet with its bulletin boards and Usenet groups that had pre-dated the web. You could access both through the web, but there was precious little conversation.

That did begin to change. There were sites like Bianca's Smut Shack, which inhabited bianca.com and was the web's first chat room, launching in 1994. Forums followed soon after, which allowed users to sign up and talk with others asynchronously.

There was also IRC, which was a chat-based system that had been around since 1988. However, IRC was the preserve mostly

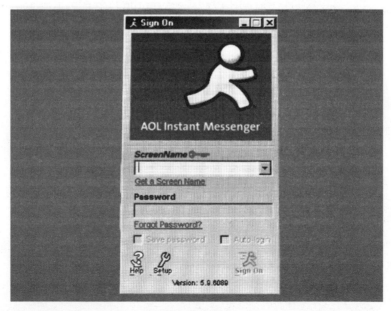

The AOL sign-on screen, a familiar sight for many.

of the tech-literate and remained beyond the reach of others because it had the cache of being mostly for nerds. ICQ, an Israeli instant messaging program that used the internet to provide real-time communication with friends, arrived in November 1996, while the yellow running man icon of AOL Instant Messenger, or AIM, became a mainstay on any teenager's desktop in May 1997. MSN Messenger was Microsoft's answer to demand for an instant messenger and became popular after its release in 1999.

Forums and chat programs were the early equivalents of social media, allowing users to interact and converse through the internet, even if you were miles away from one another.

But for all the benefits of the early web in bringing people together, expanding individuals' horizons and teaching them new things, there were drawbacks. There always are.

The first spam email

Those early days of the web were a demonstration in utopian adherence to the rules. Generally, the first adopters of this new technology were conscious of the power they had been given – and they deployed it wisely. They self-regulated. At times, they sacrificed personal interest for the greater good. They self-policed, with anyone being too boisterous on Usenet groups told to pipe down, or downplayed.

But as with anything, one bad apple can quickly spoil the bunch. Or in this case, two bad apples.

Laurence Canter and Martha Siegel were immigration attorneys based in Phoenix, Arizona. The married couple realized the power of the internet to reach a vast number of people in a short space of time – and the potential business opportunity of being seen by so many people. By the mid-1990s, the Internet Society, which tracked the growth of the internet, estimated that 25 million people had logged on.

So, in early 1994, they hit upon a plan. They'd harness the community-building power of the internet to market their wares.

They developed a computer script – a bit of code that automates onerous, time-consuming tasks – to send out mass messages to more than 5,500 Usenet groups. On 12 April 1994, they hit send on their message through the script, called Masspost.

The message was a confusing one for many of the Usenet groups in which it landed:

Green Card Lottery 1994 May Be The Last One!

THE DEADLINE HAS BEEN ANNOUNCED.

The Green Card Lottery is a completely legal program giving away a certain annual allotment of Green Cards to persons born in certain countries. The lottery program was scheduled to continue on a permanent basis. However, recently, Senator Alan J Simpson introduced a bill into the U. S. Congress which could end any future lotteries. THE 1994 LOTTERY IS SCHEDULED TO TAKE PLACE SOON, BUT IT MAY BE THE VERY LAST ONE.

PERSONS BORN IN MOST COUNTRIES QUALIFY, MANY FOR FIRST TIME.

The only countries NOT qualifying are: Mexico; India; P.R. China; Taiwan, Philippines, North Korea, Canada, United Kingdom (except Northern Ireland), Jamaica, Domican [sic] Republic, El Salvador and Vietnam.

Lottery registration will take place soon. 55,000 Green Cards will be given to those who register correctly. NO JOB IS REQUIRED.

THERE IS A STRICT JUNE DEADLINE. THE TIME TO START IS NOW!!

For FREE information via Email, send request to cslaw@ indirect.com

For some Usenet groups, focused on the interests of newly arrived immigrants to the United States or those seeking permanent residency in the US, the missive might have been useful. But for members of alt.fan.ronald-reagan, who encountered the message just after 9.30 a.m. on 12 April, it was likely puzzling. Spare a thought for those on the alt.snowmobiles server, who saw the message fifteen minutes later as Masspost worked its way through its list, or for participants on the alt.sex.masturbation Usenet group, who got it around the same time.

The first denial of service attack

Ardent fans of rock band The Grateful Dead who gathered on rec.music.gdead were among many who began to think of a way to wreak their revenge on Canter and Siegel. Alongside pointing out that the majority of internet users at the time wouldn't be the people needing green cards, users and fans like Ron Kalmbacher suggested swamping the lawyers with emailed questions to give them a taste of their own medicine. Chuck Narad, another music fan, sent them around 200 separate messages of his own.

The sentiment of those early internet adopters to the first commercial spam message was best summed up by Howard Rheingold, who told *TIME* magazine that it was like opening up his mailbox to find 'a letter, two bills and 60,000 pieces of junk mail'.

The internet got its own back. 'We sent so much email back to them, we took down their server,' said Leonard Kleinrock, one of the engineers involved in sending the very first message on ARPANET, back in 1969. As a consequence of the first spam message, the internet inadvertently created the first denial of service attack – where a website or service is taken offline by directing an impossibly large amount of traffic to it.

The response was a fascinating study in the mass human response and could itself be studied as the first case of an internet pile-on – but Kleinrock, who helped usher in the internet era, was concerned. 'The important point is the cat was now out of the bag,' he said. 'This created an enormous change in the philosophy, the view, the mentality of what this network was for. This was now a marketplace. It was now a money-making machine. We can reach the consumer. We can extract money and make it a profit-making business.'

We're still living in the unenviable shadow of that first spam message today, believes Kleinrock. As for the two lawyers who sent that first message, which would be called 'spam' for its low quality (a phrase first coined a year earlier thanks to an accidental sharing of 200 messages onto a Usenet group by a user called Richard Depew), they claimed to have drummed up $100,000 in new business from their mass message. The duo wrote a book published in 1996, titled *How to Make a Fortune on the Internet Superhighway*.

But it wouldn't last. Karma caught up with Canter, the husband of the spam duo. In 1997, the lawyer was disbarred by the Supreme Court of Tennessee. The reason? 'Just to emphasize that his email campaign was a particularly egregious offence,' said William W. Hunt III of the Tennessee Board of Professional Responsibility.

Canter wasn't the only one to launch such attacks – and a new generation of denial of service attacks, which were distributed by co-opting unsuspecting victims into being the attackers themselves, would follow.

The first major DDoS attack – and internet reliability

For something so reliant on sometimes temperamental hardware that has occasionally been haphazardly layered on top of other bits, the internet has surprisingly few hiccups. When sites go offline, even if only for a matter of minutes, it tends to make the news – highlighting how unusual it is.

Sometimes those outages are down to innocent human error, as with Twitter's intermittent 2023 outages as overworked staff were asked to enact difficult changes with little of the institutional knowledge required to do so. Sometimes they're accidents – like when undersea cables are accidentally cut by trawlers dragging anchor along the seabed. But sometimes they're deliberate.

In 2000, Michael Calce was a high-school student in Quebec, Canada, who went by the online username Mafiaboy. Calce, then fifteen, was always keen to cause trouble. He was part of a group of hackers online called TNT, and he loved computers – so in February that year, he came up with a plan he called Rivolta (or 'rebellion' in Italian). It would bombard the servers hosting Yahoo's website with a distributed denial of service (DDoS) attack. The plan worked: Yahoo was taken offline for an hour, as were the websites of Amazon, CNN, Dell, E*Trade and eBay.

'The New York Stock Exchange, they were freaking out, because they were all investing in these e-commerce companies,' he recalled to NPR. It was at the time one of the biggest DDoS attacks in history – and it earned Calce his own page in the internet archives. It also drew the attention of authorities, who gave him an eight-month sentence in open custody, despite his age.

The first major internet virus

Calce joined the ranks of internet rogues, but he was far from the first. For decades, people have been seeking to break the internet with almost as much determination as they have been trying to build it.

Robert Morris was one of those who fell into the former category – a hacker, rather than a builder. His family was intrinsically intertwined with the internet: his father had worked for Bell Labs before becoming chief scientist for the National Computer Security Center, which operated within the US National Security Agency, and, following in his footsteps, Robert was a Harvard computer science graduate, who went by 'RTM' online.

Around 8.30 p.m. on 2 November 1988, Morris set off a computer program that would later be called the Morris Worm. Friends of his say he didn't mean to do anything malicious: he had found a handful of security vulnerabilities on systems running Unix, an operating system Morris knew well, and decided to see if he could exploit it.

Morris's worm was intended to sneak its way through those vulnerabilities and rampage around the internet, not causing harm. But he coded it incorrectly, meaning that rather than doing no harm it ended up slowing the internet to a halt. The FBI estimates that Morris caused at least $100,000, and potentially millions of dollars, of damage to the internet – which today would be equivalent to $250,000 or more.

Morris undertook efforts to hide his tracks: a recently arrived Cornell student after his Harvard graduation, he hacked into

SQL Slammer worm (2003)

Morris's worm was the first virus to hit the internet, but it would be far from the last. While ransomware attacks, which hold user data hostage unless money is paid to the attackers in the form of cryptocurrencies, dominate the world of cyberattacks today, back in 2003 things were altogether simpler. A computer virus that contained just 376 bytes of code managed to bring down ATM networks, delay the printing of newspapers and slow the internet to a crawl.

This was the SQL Slammer, and it was a foundational moment in the history of the internet. People first realized things were wrong on 25 January 2003, when worldwide internet systems ground to a halt. Routers were becoming swamped with requests to send and receive packets of data from servers that had been infected with the SQL Slammer, a tiny virus that took advantage of a security vulnerability in Microsoft's SQL Server.

Any server running the vulnerable software would be infected with a self-replicating virus that then created new versions, which it sent out onto the internet in search of new IP addresses with the same vulnerability. If it found one, the action would be repeated.

The SQL Slammer spread so quickly that most of its 75,000 vulnerable servers were hit within ten minutes. It proved that computer servers needed constant updating to keep ahead of bad actors.

a computer based at the Massachusetts Institute of Technology to hit send on the worm. Only when things went wrong did he fess up to being behind the virus.

The student's reticence to admit to what he had done was because it was a crime – literally. In 1986, Congress had passed the Computer Fraud and Abuse Act, making it a crime to break into computers like he had done. Morris was convicted in 1989 – the first person to be convicted under the law. He was given a fine and 400 hours of community service for his wrongdoing. He ended up becoming a professor at MIT, the place he hacked into to launch his worm.

The first online banner ad

For almost as long as we've had the internet, we've been sold to through it. From the first spam email trying to hawk us immigration services and support to gain a green card, to the ubiquitous Instagram ads that follow us around today, almost all of our actions in a digital world are just waiting to be commoditized.

That bombardment by marketing messages means that increasingly we turn to tools to drown out the noise. Four in ten of us regularly use adblockers on our web browsers – bits of software that use computer code to recognize adverts on websites and stop them from loading.

But there was a time when people willingly clicked on adverts – in fact, seeing them was a novelty and something you'd seek out, akin to making a pilgrimage to a well-known and beloved tourist attraction.

The first ever advert on the internet when it arrived, then, was a major moment. It popped up on hotwired.com, one of the web's coolest places to be, on 27 October 1994, and it stayed up for four

Banner ads would soon take over the internet – as you can see here.

months. It was placed there by US telecoms company AT&T, and it wasn't much to look at.

It was a thin, horizontal strip of black, upon which was superimposed eight simple words, coloured in a glitzy, glittery kaleidoscope of shades: 'Have you ever clicked your mouse right here?'

There was an arrow in the same garish combination of colours that led to the right, pointing to text that said: 'You will'. It was tiny: 476 pixels wide, by 56 high.

The braggadocious claim that users would click on such an advert would be laughable today. But back then people did. Some 44 per cent of those who saw the advert clicked on it, taking them to AT&T's website, where they could learn more. The novelty was too great not to.

However, it quickly wore off. Once it was proven that banner ads worked, they were plastered everywhere on the web. It quickly became a problem, choking up vital data on slow internet connections. The world's first ad blocker, called Internet Fast Forward, was released in 1996 by half a dozen programmers in Chapel Hill, North Carolina, trading under the name PrivNet, to try to tackle the scourge of ads.

And they were a scourge. Even the children of Joe McCambley, who helped design that first banner ad for AT&T in 1994, told him his work was 'like inventing smallpox'.

Sex sells

Since the dawn of humankind, sex has been at the forefront of people's minds. Cave drawings depicted illicit acts; Roman mosaics, still intact, show people in flagrante. And so, as soon as the internet came to be, it was obvious that sex would be on it.

At first, those images weren't images at all. The low bandwidth and slow connection speeds meant anything outside of text wasn't possible. But as we'll learn in Chapter 5, with the arrival of the emoticon and its younger sibling, the emoji, there are ways to depict images without using images at all.

ASCII art has long been a mainstay of the internet. For the uninitiated, ASCII is short for the American Standard Code for Information Interchange, a standardized series of symbols that would regulate how people communicated through computer text. The need for such a standard was first identified in 1961; two years later, the first edition was developed. It included the letters of the alphabet and numbers, as well as a series of symbols, from brackets to dashes, dollar signs to arrows.

Soon enough, people realized that if you put some of those symbols together, you could create 'drawings' of sorts – much in the same way the Romans realized you can cement together tiny fragments of tiles to create a broader image. ASCII art became a thing.

ASCII art of three rabbits.

And as with any form of art, the gaze soon turned to nudes and depictions of sex acts. ASCII porn quickly followed, where artistic users put their skills to portraying compromising situations. That was soon outmoded by people downloading binary files – instructions for their computer to compile a picture – from Usenet groups and then bringing them together offline on their own computers, using specialized software. Binary files were smaller than images, but when put together they could depict the same images we now take for granted online.

Despite being involved in some of the earliest expressions of sex online, Stephen Cohen (see box opposite) wasn't the person who laid claim to what would become prime internet real estate: the domain name Sex.com.

Instead, it was an enterprising entrepreneur called Gary Kremen. Kremen realized that people in the early days of home computing didn't know how to use their computers, and so he built a business selling discs full of software that he found online. Soon enough, Kremen also started packaging pornographic pictures alongside the software, meeting market demand. (Kremen would later set up dating site Match.com, as we'll learn in Chapter 5.)

Kremen used his business acumen to look beyond the here and now in the early days of the World Wide Web, seeing it would be

Ooh la la

Simultaneously, some decided they didn't need images to get their kicks: they just needed text-based interactions with like-minded people. Stephen Cohen was one such person: a self-confessed criminal always looking for the next big money-making scheme. Cohen ran the Los Angeles Free Love Society, a mail-order catalogue of members of a club looking for casual sex in the mid-1960s. But it was mostly a scam: most of the members were men who paid $20 out of lust, getting nothing but a lighter wallet in return.

Cohen was also involved in the internet in its formative years on bulletin board systems, or BBSes. In the summer of 1979, he sought to combine his two interests – computers and sex – by launching the French Connection BBS.

Chosen for its exotic connotations, the name French Connection allowed users to indulge their wildest fantasies through text. The interactions eventually spread offline, involving sex parties in monied parts of California. It was one of the first places on the burgeoning internet that people could explore their sexuality.

possible to make money not just by offering services or launching businesses but by accumulating items that would be imbued with worth as the World Wide Web evolved.

This is how he came to register Sex.com on 9 May 1994, by sending an email and a letter to the Herndon, Virginia, offices of Network Solutions Inc. (NSI), a technology company that had been given sole jurisdiction over granting the rights to domain names – the letters and numbers you type into an address bar in order to direct your web browser to a particular website.

NSI had been given the contract to oversee the disbursement of domain names to applicants by the US Defense Information Systems Agency, which had quickly realized in the early 1990s that this was going to become an onerous task (by 1991, 12,000 domain names had been registered; today there are hundreds of millions).

Sex.com

Kremen wasn't specifically focused on Sex.com – his letter registering that domain name was an afterthought, the end of a long list of domain names he chose to register in his name after flicking through the classified section of a copy of the *San Francisco Bay Guardian* to understand what things people were interested in.

The list was relatively long not because Kremen had deep pockets but because, unlike now, when domain names can change hands for millions of dollars – LasVegas.com was bought in 2005 from a private owner for a deal worth $90 million over a number of years – in the early 1990s you didn't have to pay to register a domain name with the authorities. They would just give you it. A *WIRED* journalist asked for, and earned the rights to, McDonalds.com in early 1994 before approaching the company to ask them if they wanted it. The fast-food giant was nonplussed but was eventually convinced to give the journalist $3,500 for the rights. By September 1995, NSI, which had since been bought by Science Applications International Corp., realized they could charge for the rights. They began levying a $5 registration fee for every domain name. Within six months, they made close to $20 million.

Before the fees were enacted, Kremen dutifully applied for the rights to Sex.com and was granted it – with no outlay except for the price of the stamp for his letter to NSI. The site remained dormant until October 1995, when Stephen Cohen came across the URL and noticed it was empty. He called Kremen and claimed that he should be given the rights to it – citing, without evidence, that he had rights over the Sex.com trademark because of his history with the French Connection BBS.

When Kremen gave him short shrift, Cohen stole the domain, falsifying documents with the registration organization, who handed it over to him, no questions asked. Cohen began pasting Sex.com with wall-to-wall banner adverts.

Cohen began selling adverts on Sex.com for $50,000 a time, with analysts valuing the site's worth at $100 million or more. But it was all based on a con – and one that Gary Kremen was the victim of.

A years' long legal battle over the ownership of the domain name would ensue, which returned Sex.com to Kremen on 27 November 2000. The court also decreed that Cohen owed Kremen tens of millions of dollars – which was never paid.

Kremen never wanted to be in the pornography business, so after much soul-searching he offloaded Sex.com to another company, for $14 million on 20 January 2006. It was declared 'a landmark deal' by news coverage at the time.

The first OnlyFans before OnlyFans

Today, millions of people make a living selling access to themselves – and, often, pictures of themselves in compromising positions – through OnlyFans. The subscription website allows avid fans to pay to access exclusive content posted by creators, frequently pornographic. OnlyFans was founded in 2016, but more than twenty years earlier, an enterprising stripper realized how to capitalize on the devoted nature of her fanbase.

Danni Ashe was a Seattle-based stripper who decided to take

some light reading material with her on a 1995 beach holiday: a book on HTML programming. HTML was a key part of coding any website in the early days of the World Wide Web.

Using what she learned from the book, Ashe launched her own website – Danni's Hard Drive – the same year. She posted pictures, videos and audio interviews that people could pay $15 a month to access. The model, as OnlyFans and others who followed in Ashe's footsteps quickly learned, worked. She ended up making $6.5 million a year, and it was claimed that the number of people downloading content from her website accounted for more bandwidth usage than the entirety of Central America.

While some were going legit with porn, there was also an undercurrent of porn piracy.

Sex has long ruled the internet – but it has also posed tricky questions for those online about the ethics of sharing content with a wider audience. A sex tape recorded by *Baywatch* star Pamela Anderson and her then husband Tommy Lee was stolen from their home in 1995 and quickly found its way onto the internet. It became one of the earliest viral sensations and caused Anderson enormous distress. It was in many ways the first example of the non-consensual sharing of intimate images – something that continues to plague the internet, which never forgets, today.

Online piracy

For as long as people have been making art, people have been making copies of art. From cheap knock-offs of paintings by the old masters to the scourge of home taping that threatened the music and movie industries, piracy has long been a part of our daily lives.

But the internet, like many things, helped to supercharge piracy. Online, the early pirates were involved in what's called the warez scene – an underground subculture that originated from the BBSes that existed before the World Wide Web, before moving over to Internet Relay Chat messaging services in the late 1980s and to web-adjacent methods called FTP (file transfer protocol) servers in the 1990s.

If you were to log on to the early pirate BBSes, servers and chat rooms, you'd see two main things being traded: software and porn. Enterprising users with access to flatbed scanners would copy in the latest *Playboy* centrefolds then trade them online; likewise, nerds looking for the latest software would offer to trade bootleg versions of popular programs. It became such an issue that the Software Publishers Association, an industry body, launched a public awareness campaign called Don't Copy That Floppy, which saw schoolchildren across the United States watch a videotape, including a rap, exhorting people not to engage in software piracy.

Still, in the pre-internet era, you had to know someone who knew someone – or know where to look and what to ask – to find pirated materials. You needed friends who travelled to Hong Kong, where pirated video games and movies were in abundance, or a friendly shop assistant at the home video store who would slip you an illicit copy of a video tape under the counter, if you explained in the right way what you were looking for. But the internet brought piracy into the mainstream – eventually.

Even in the 1990s, you still had to have the right contacts. Search engines were still relatively rudimentary, and most entries into the world of piracy would come through personal introductions: someone in the scene, perhaps a user of a piracy BBS or IRC channel, would let you know where to find an Aladdin's cave of illicit material.

People tend to pirate content to save cash: a 1994 survey in a business ethics journal found that people pirated software because of the cost – the results repeated in a 1997 study. After all, what can compete with free? As Perry Barlow, the founder of the Electronic Frontier Foundation, wrote in a 1994 *WIRED* article on the internet: 'Everything you know about intellectual property is wrong.'

Both those surveys pre-dated the rise of the single program that would change piracy forever – and which would get ordinary people used to the idea of not paying for things.

Napster is born

The year was 1999, and Shawn Fanning and Sean Parker had big plans. Fanning was a freshman at Northeastern University who was growing restless. In January, he dropped out of his studies to spend more time coding a platform he believed could solve a problem would-be pirates had long had: they'd spend hours trying to download individual music tracks on sluggish internet connections from websites and IRC channels, only to see their attempts fail before the transfer was completed.

Fanning had used the name 'napster' on chat rooms and some time in 1998 revealed that he had a plan to fix that bugbear: peer-to-peer connection and transfer. The idea was that you could make available certain folders on your computer that people could access through the internet. They could then download the file from your computer at a pace their internet connection could handle. There'd be no risks of timeouts or failed downloads. You could pause and recommence downloads at your leisure. Better yet, you could search through the entirety of the database of MP3 files available to download. (The MP3 was a file format first released in 1991. It managed to crunch down a data-heavy audio file into a more manageable file size for slow internet connections by getting rid of bits in the song that are outside the ability of most people to hear. It's like wiping the background from a sketch, so you only see the

A screenshot of Napster, dating from 2001.

bits that are important.) Napster was like having a catalogue of illegally obtained material in your hands.

Parker happened to be in the same chat room and was enthralled by the idea. The two endeavoured to team up and release Napster – which they did on 1 June 1999. By October that year, users had granted access to more than 4 million files their peers could download – all for free – which gained the attention and raised the ire of the music industry. This was years before the arrival of iTunes, which launched on 28 April 2003, and the ability to legally download MP3 files. (iTunes launched with 200,000 tracks available to download.) Three years later, streaming service Spotify launched, eventually eradicating the need to buy individual songs.

Napster was flouting the law. The Digital Millennium Copyright Act (DMCA) was passed in October 1998 and became effective two years later. It allowed copyright holders to doggedly pursue and seek damages – plus jail time – from those found to be handling illegally obtained content.

The music industry was right to be worried. Napster took piracy out of the shadows and firmly into the mainstream. Some university internet connection administrators reported between 40 per cent and 60 per cent of all traffic going through their networks was MP3 file transfers, through Napster and a number of competitors that operated in a similar way. The search term 'MP3' overtook 'sex' for the first time ever in the spring of 1999, right as Napster launched. By 2001, Napster's 70 million users worldwide were downloading 300 billion MP3s a year.

The MP3s available on Napster covered all genres and a bevy of artists; Metallica sued the platform in March 2000, after it found a demo version of one of its songs, 'I Disappear', was accessible through the service before it was officially released. The same thing happened to Madonna's August 2000 song 'Music', which hit Napster more than two months before it was meant to be heard by the world, and Radiohead found some tracks from their album *Kid A* appeared online months before the CD was released.

It wasn't just artists who were chasing down Napster in court. Eighteen different record labels clubbed together to launch *A&M Records* v. *Napster*, which issued an injunction on 5 March 2001, stopping Napster from allowing people to swap copyrighted music through the service. It took more than four months for Napster to comply, with the service shutting down illegal downloads on 11 July 2001. The company behind Napster settled its lawsuit for $26 million.

Napster tried to go straight. It provided a paid-for subscription service for licensed music, but users accustomed to getting stuff for free balked at paying up. At the same time, record labels who had spent two years seeing Napster as the enemy weren't overly enamoured with the idea of trusting the company with their files. Those users who did pay the subscription didn't have a huge range of tracks to choose from. Napster filed for bankruptcy in June 2002.

By then, though, a raft of other apps using similar technology had arrived: there was LimeWire, which was founded in 2000 by former Wall Street trader Mark Gorton and by 2007 was installed on one in three computers worldwide. There was also KaZaA, developed by Estonian programmers and launched in March 2001. Most of these children of Napster were sued out of existence. But it was too late: the world had gotten a taste for free content. A totally different method of peer-to-peer file transfer, called BitTorrent, had also been unveiled on 2 July 2001, which remains one of the main methods of accessing files you haven't paid for today.

Entertainment strikes back

The entertainment industry's response to the rise of illegal piracy, which saw US music sales drop from $14.6 billion a year in 1999 to $6.3 billion in 2009, was to meet the pirates halfway. They realized people were no longer buying physical copies of music when they could access MP3s and play them on their brand new MP3 players (Apple's iPod was released in October 2001).

So they started selling MP3s. But they weren't the same MP3s people had been pirating for years: these MP3s included digital rights management (DRM).

DRM headed off the big risk rights holders feared: that unauthorized versions of their products – whether music, movies or software – could be spread via the internet. DRM allowed them to dip their toe into the online waters, distributing media and software through the internet, but also to control tightly what happened to their work once it was let loose. It was computer code

Piracy gets one up

The new restrictions didn't wash for consumers used to rights-free access to music and other files. So, a new revolution in piracy began. In 2003, The Pirate Bay, a piracy website that connected users to downloadable torrent files they could access through BitTorrent, was launched from a computer server co-opted by Gottfrid Svartholm, a Swedish hacker working for a company in Mexico, whose bosses had little idea of what he was doing.

As its popularity boomed, The Pirate Bay's borrowing of the company's servers became more obvious, and so the site's hosting moved to Sweden. By the end of 2004, The Pirate Bay was linking more than a million peer-to-peer connections, which were transferring 60,000 torrent files. That became 2.5 million peers by the end of 2005, before a Swedish police raid in May 2006. Still, The Pirate Bay lived on – and continues to do so, dodging bans and threats.

that would limit what could be done with a file once it was in the ownership of everyday people.

Though it was a popular solution to the problem of piracy in the 2000s, its origins were much older. Electronic Publishing Resources was the creator of what would now be considered DRM software – and its founder Victor Shear came up with it in 1986 to help sell one of his own products. Shear was in charge of a company selling database management software to libraries, which were starting to get into lending CD-ROMs to users. But the makers of those CD-ROMs were wary of letting libraries get their hands on their products, because the fear was that there was

Even those within the music industry use the platform: in 2016, Kanye West tweeted a picture of his laptop screen, showing a web browser open to a number of sites. The image was meant to show how he was progressing on his new album. But what West didn't realize was that users could also see he had tabs open on his web browser, apparently to a torrent of music-making software and a website that allowed users to take the audio from YouTube files – again, illegally.

At the same time, other sites came and went, including Oink's Pink Palace, which was a private music site funded through donations by its users, which ran from 2004 until 2007. When it was shut down due to an attempted prosecution for copyright fraud (which Alan Ellis, the owner, was found not guilty of), a replacement cropped up called What.CD. That lasted nearly a decade before it too shut down, in 2016, to pre-empt a police raid.

little incentive for people who had already borrowed a CD-ROM to then go out and purchase the same thing.

The tool was initially called ROI, or return on investment, which was at the forefront of Shear's patent application in 1986. That patent launched Electronic Publishing Resources, and soon Shear's idea of a digital rights management tool was being developed by many other competitors. Shear went on to found a different company, InterTrust, that hawked DRM-style tools to companies beginning to worry about the wild-west attitude to copyright on the internet.

InterTrust owned a number of patents around DRM, and

Shear himself was motivated by 'developing the basis for a civil society in cyberspace', one former employee said. That civility didn't extend to protecting the rights to his patents, however: Shear sued Microsoft for infringing on said patents and settled for $440 million. Shear's ideas basically became the norm for a wave of new DRM tools, which rights holders loved but everyday users loathed because of how much they locked down the ability to do, well … anything with digital files.

The dot-com boom and bust

While plenty of people sought to steal content without making money, many businesses on the growing internet managed to make lots of cash regardless. The companies that had first-mover advantage were able to reap enormous rewards and froth up the market with blockbuster valuations and initial public offerings (IPOs) to the stock markets.

Those internet-based companies helped the Nasdaq stock index rise more than 800 per cent between 1995 and March 2000. In part, that's because the number of internet-based companies ballooned: an estimated 50,000 companies were founded between 1996 and 2000, backed by more than a quarter of a trillion dollars in venture capital, around the online ecosystem. Nearly 250 internet companies launched an IPO in 1999. Morgan Stanley tracked a basket of 199 already launched internet stocks, which it said were worth $450 billion in October 1999.

It seemed like there was a 100 per cent success rate when it came to being an internet start-up: simply being online was a licence to print money. Venture capitalists, who control vast volumes of cash and seek massive returns, were all too happy to support new start-ups based in the web hotbed of Silicon Valley, California. It didn't matter if they weren't yet making money. And they weren't.

Those 199 companies tracked by Morgan Stanley worth nearly half a trillion dollars? They sold just $21 billion worth of goods every year. And not for a profit: their combined losses were actually $6.2 billion.

One journalist covering the dot-com boom later told *Vanity Fair* that at parties funded by the cash from venture investment, founders barely out of college would confidently answer questions about whether they were profitable, saying that they were 'pre-revenue companies'. (It's an issue that would persist throughout the history of Big Tech companies. Around four in five companies that launched an IPO in the 1980s were profitable when they floated on stock markets. By 2019, just one in five start-ups valued at more than $1 billion were actually profitable.)

The implication was that they would eventually get to the point of making money – a model that tech start-ups today still pursue, of growth at all costs in the hope that they can find a workable business model before they burn through their cash. And journalists weren't always asking the right questions. *WIRED* was keen to big up the best of the dot-com boom. In one July 1997 article, reporters wrote:

> We have entered a period of sustained growth that could eventually double the world's economy every dozen years and bring increasing prosperity for – quite literally – billions of people on the planet. We are riding the early waves of a twenty-five-year run of a greatly expanding economy that will do much to solve seemingly intractable problems like poverty and to ease tensions throughout the world.

It was a haughty, portentous claim.

But, of course, it wasn't true.

How the wild west was won

The twin narratives outlined in this chapter highlight the anarchic nature of Web 1.0. In a matter of years, we moved from a folksy internet where people gathered on forums and chat apps and tended to their personal websites on a small, difficult to discover corner of the web, to one where big platforms dominated.

That Big Tech presence was total. The do-it-yourself approach that had exemplified the web's first near-decade of existence was still present, but it was being swarmed and swamped by the dominance of a few big names.

Netscape Navigator, the techy, tinkering web browser beloved by hobbyists and early adopters, was being supplanted by Internet Explorer, the behemoth designed to be inescapable and irreplaceable on users' computers. The personal home pages of those who had carefully crafted their online presence began to look dated and kitschy as the web became big business. In their place were a handful of bigger sites – many of which we'll look at in the next chapter – in whose gravitational pull every other website orbited.

Things were changing, and they were changing fast. One epoch was ending. Another was just getting started.

Chapter 3
Web 2.0

Welcome Web 2.0

By the end of the 1990s, the World Wide Web was becoming widespread. More people were coming online thanks to cheap or free connections to the internet, while the cost of the hardware that would help them access the web was coming down in price. In the United States, they were even giving it away: it was possible to buy an internet-connected PC from manufacturer eMachines for free, if you took into account in-store rebates and signed up to a contract with an ISP.

As the millennium dawned, more than four in ten people in North America were online, and one in eight in Europe and central Asia. The Western world was moving online, and fast – but that didn't reflect the entire global picture. Worldwide, just under 7 per cent of people were connected to the internet, underlining that where someone lives is largely the responsible factor in their access to the internet.

Nevertheless, this was a new era. And fittingly, it needed a new name.

That came from user experience designer Darcy DiNucci, who wrote a story for *PRINT* magazine's April 1999 issue, titled 'Fragmented Future'. In the article, DiNucci wrote:

> The relationship of Web 1.0 to the Web of tomorrow is roughly
> the equivalence of Pong to The Matrix ... The Web we know
> now, which loads into a browser window in essentially static
> screenfuls, is only an embryo of the Web to come.

She forecast a future that was not on the horizon but which was already here, and it would be called Web 2.0. It would 'fragment into countless permutations with different looks, behaviors, uses, and hardware hosts'. It would be interactive. It would be on our TV sets, our phones and maybe our microwaves (an augur of the internet of things, or IoT).

It was prescient. It was a new age. Its name would even be borrowed for the title of a conference that started in 2004. But it was also an epoch that would see landgrabs from some of Web 1.0's biggest names and a giant battle for control, the impact of which we're still living through today.

Web 2.0 was an exciting time for us all. But to tell the story of how we got there, we need to go back to the 1.0 era.

The dot-com bubble bursts

The fever of the dot-com boom couldn't last. The numbers just didn't add up. AOL was riding atop the wave: in the 1990s, its stock had increased in value by 80,000 per cent. It merged with Time Warner on 10 January 2000 to create what AOL CEO Steve Case said would be 'the global company of the internet age'.

In reality, the merger would be a failure. As the twentieth century became the twenty-first, the dot-com boom was about to hit a brick wall. But the world wasn't to know that yet.

No single company perhaps better exemplifies the issue of the dot-com boom and bust than Pets.com – a company that sold popular pet supplies. Launched by Greg McLemore, the idea behind the business was a smart one. People love their pets, and they're willing to spend money on them.

The smart idea stopped there. McLemore wasn't the only one who noticed that gap in the market, so Pets.com was competing against a range of other businesses. Still, McLemore was convincing, selling Amazon a 54 per cent stake in the company shortly after it launched in February 1999. Pets.com IPO'd successfully in February 2000, raising $82.5 million.

The reason why is a puzzle. Pets.com had shared in its IPO prospectus its 1999 sales figures. It had only sold $5.7 million worth of products. Meanwhile, it had lost $61 million on that. The maths didn't add up.

Why became more obvious when you looked at the business model. Pets.com lost 57 cents on every single dollar of sales. It charged $5 to ship a massive bag of dog food, half the price it cost the company to send it. In the dot-com boom, the business model didn't matter; all people cared about was the perception. You could fake it until you made it.

Except Pets.com didn't. Just 268 days after it launched on the stock exchange, it entered liquidation. It wasn't the first. Nor would it be the last.

The dot-com bubble bursting saw a retrenchment in some of the web's biggest names. But there was no stopping Web 2.0's massive expansion – and something needed to be done to navigate it.

The world of search

The ever-expanding borders of the World Wide Web produced a problem for those who chose to 'surf' it, as the early terminology had it. It was just too big.

When the World Wide Web project launched on 6 August 1991 as the brainchild of Tim Berners-Lee, it had a single website: his own, hosted at info.cern.ch, explaining the concept. By 1992, there were ten websites for early browsers to get their brains around. By the time 1993 rolled around, the web had expanded to 130 sites – just about enough to remember in one person's head.

But by the start of 1994, things were getting out of hand. There were more than 25 million users online, who could navigate 2,738 websites, each of which could contain many separate web pages. While that was exciting for the early navigators of the web, it also made finding things tricky. Trying to remember exactly where you'd seen that amazing bit of information a few hours ago when you'd since navigated to hundreds of other websites was a challenge.

Getting lost was becoming an issue – as was information retrieval. This is what the two Stanford University students behind Yahoo, Jerry Yang and David Filo, recognized. They set up what we might now think of as a search engine but was really more of a digital filing cabinet designed to try to divide up the web into distinct categories. There were sections for News and Media, for Society and Culture, and for Entertainment. There was at first, at least on Yahoo's home page, no text box into which you could type what you were looking for. Instead there was a sea of links, categorized into subsections.

Initially, Yahoo wasn't called that: it was 'Jerry and David's Guide to the World Wide Web'. The duo renamed it Yahoo, an acronym for 'Yet Another Hierarchical Officious Oracle', when they came to recognize that it would have more use than just their own personal interest.

Their revelation wasn't exactly original. Attempts to categorize and help people find information on the internet in a less haphazard way pre-dated Yahoo's founding in January 1994. There was Archie, launched in 1990, which sought to list all the file directories hosted on the internet, then Veronica, designed by researchers in Nevada, and Jughead, another one. (The latter two were a tribute to the former: Veronica and Jughead are characters in the *Archie* series of comics.) None was a search engine in the sense we'd know them as now, however.

Berners-Lee at one point even tried to keep track of all the new servers popping up on the World Wide Web, presented in reverse chronological order of when they went online. But the task soon proved too challenging.

Because of that enormous leap in website numbers between the start of 1993 and 1994, 1993 turned out to be the real genesis of what we'd now recognize as web search. That year, committed hobbyists looking to index the internet began trying different ways of collating their information.

JumpStation is born

The argument for search engines was not a difficult one to make. 'We need to be able to specify exactly what we need and let computers do our searching for us,' wrote Paul Glister in a 1995 book subtitled, 'The Essential Guide to the Internet Interface'. But how to do it was not so simple.

The person who came up with what we'd now consider the key principles behind how most of our modern-day search engines work – sending so-called web crawlers out into the digital world and seeing what has changed, bringing back information that can then be categorized and presented in response to a text search – was a computer science graduate at the University of Stirling, called Jonathon Fletcher. Fletcher planned to study for his PhD but couldn't fund his studies, so instead he took a job at the university.

Fletcher wanted to try to get a sense of what was out there on the web, so he sent out an army of web crawlers, or computer robots, which started from a list of URLs Fletcher supplied them and followed each hyperlink on every page to find new pages on other websites. When a crawler encountered a web page it didn't have in its database, it recorded and stored the page's title, URL and a brief summary of its contents, based on any headers used on the website.

Those first crawlers were sent out onto the World Wide Web on 12 December 1993. By 21 December, they had exhausted the entire web that they could index, returning with around 25,000 results. (The process would be constantly repeated; by June 1994, it was 275,000 web pages. Remember: a web page is just one section of a larger website.) JumpStation, as Fletcher called the website which allowed users to query the contents of the database his robots had gathered, was born.

Not everyone on the web was happy with the idea of a little robot scurrying around their online homes. 'Some operators thought it was invading their website, and one posted a message saying words to the effect of, "We don't know who you are or what you are doing, but please stop it,"' he told a newspaper in 2009.

Fletcher publicized his search engine through the 'What's New' page of Mosaic, which if you recall from Chapter 1 was at that point the main entry point onto the web for many users. JumpStation grew in popularity. It was nominated for, but notably didn't win, a Best of the Web Award in 1994 for 'Best Navigational Aid'. The site it lost out to, WorldWideWebWorm, was set up by Oliver McBryan, a computer science student at the University of Colorado who began work on a similar concept to JumpStation in September 1993, but it wasn't released for public use until March 1994. The Best of the Web Awards praised WorldWideWebWorm as being 'Fairly close to comprehensive already, gaining in popularity. A robot which indexes titles, url's [sic], and reference links.'

But despite being first in the case of JumpStation and best

in the case of WorldWideWebWorm, neither project would stick around. JumpStation disappeared in 1994, as Fletcher couldn't convince his university, whose servers he was using to power the tool, to keep supporting it. McBryan's attempt fizzled out too – in large part because he meant it as a research project, rather than a money-making exercise. They were soon replaced by others who were happier to seek fortune alongside providing a utility for early web users.

Enter Google

Sergey Brin and Larry Page met and became friends (slowly, because at first they found each other obnoxious) while studying at Stanford University in the 1990s. The duo were internet natives, encountering the World Wide Web in their teens and becoming naturals in navigating it. But they too saw the issue of how to discover treasure buried deep in the outer edges of the web.

They had seen the search engines out there already and thought they weren't up to snuff. Instead, they had a better solution, which would later be outlined in a December 1998 academic paper. The technology behind the company they'd call Google (a deliberate misspelling of 'googol', a number representing ten to the hundredth power) was called PageRank.

PageRank was an algorithm that helped rank search results based on the number of other web pages that linked to a given page. So, unlike previous search engine web crawlers, which would follow links from one site to another, Google incorporated backlinks – assuming that valuable websites would be ones that received lots of backlinks.

Take, for instance, a highly reputable source of original information like a news website. As it produced information, others would then take that and discuss it on forums. If a site was linked

Google from then to now

Almost immediately, Google became synonymous with search. By November 1999, the site was handling 4 million searches every single day. By the millennium, it had become the world's largest search engine, allowing users to pick from a billion URLs with every search they made in June 2000. 'Google's new gigantic index means that you can search the equivalent of a stack of paper more than 70 miles high in less than half a second,' Larry Page said at the time.

Google had become dominant. And it would remain dominant for the next two decades. A 2023 study of more than 5,600 search engine result pages between 2000 and 2020, carried out by Portuguese researchers, found that what Google shows users – and the way it shows it – has evolved slowly over time, remaining largely the same at its core, with new additions along the way. In 2008, related searches arrived, allowing users to leap from one stream of consciousness in search to another. In the 2010s, images and selected top news stories were appended to the top of some results. Knowledge Panels and Featured Snippets, which attempted to save users clicking onto pages shown in the results by bringing the answers to questions like 'How old is Brad Pitt?' to them, arrived in 2014 and 2016 respectively.

Google evolved far beyond the simple list of ten blue links that it had been in its first iteration. But it also didn't stray too far away from that vision. That doesn't mean Google stood still, though.

back to often, it would be a high-value one. It was Google's secret sauce, and the thing that would later wipe out all competition. Like JumpStation and WorldWideWebWorm, Google utilized a web crawler, going out onto the broader web and bringing back information about all the web pages it discovered.

Google's web crawler was unleashed in March 1996, starting with Page's own home page on Stanford's website. It tracked the interconnected spider's web of links around different pages and ranked them in order of importance based on the searches users conducted.

The crawl was a significant one. Taking the information the crawler found, Google launched at Stanford University in August 1996. It had indexed around 30 million web pages and had yet to attempt indexing another 30 million or so. In all, 207 gigabytes worth of data had been downloaded. It accounted for 50 per cent of all Stanford University's bandwidth at the time – a situation that quickly became infeasible.

Google.com, which would become the search engine's permanent home, was registered on 15 September 1997. It would take another year for the company to be incorporated on 4 September 1998.

Google Image Search

In the annals of internet history, two dresses bookmark key moments that came to define the way we live online. One dress was the black and blue (or should that be white and gold?) number that went viral in 2015 as a Rorschach test for one's ability to discern visual trickery. We'll learn about that in Chapter 5.

The other was a green silk chiffon dress designed by Donatella Versace and worn by musician Jennifer Lopez to the Grammy Awards in February 2000.

The image everyone was searching for of Jennifer Lopez in her green Versace dress.

The Versace dress, with a bold below-the-belly-button neckline and a slit down the leg, became an immediate topic of conversation on the internet, just as it did across office watercoolers around the world. But there was one problem: type 'Jennifer Lopez dress' into Google in February 2000 – and many did; the search query became the most popular Google had ever seen at the time – and you would encounter search results describing the dress. But you wouldn't see a picture of it.

Google had known for a while that it ought to develop an image-based search engine, but it hadn't, until the Lopez incident, realized quite how large the pent-up demand was. Google tasked Huican Zhu, a recent hire straight out of college, and Susan Wojcicki, a product manager who would later become CEO of YouTube, to develop the tool. It was launched in July 2001 and served up image-based results taken from a corpus of 250 million indexed images in its database, in response to text-based prompts.

Ten years later, reverse image search was revealed by Google, allowing you to insert an image of your own and see where it might have come from – something that would help a legion of internet sleuths deduce mysteries and which gave birth to the OSINT (open-source intelligence) industry that, among other things, identifies Russian plots to assassinate opposition activists and attributes war crimes to their perpetrators. It's all thanks to J-Lo.

The best April Fool's joke

Not content with upending how we searched, on April Fool's Day 2004 Google took aim at revolutionizing how we use another key component of our online lives: email.

As the internet moved out of the sole purview of university computer labs and into the wider world, email addresses, which were an important part of communication online, began being distributed by ISPs. If you connected to the internet with AOL, you'd get an @aol.com email address. If your ISP, like mine in the early 2000s, was Freeserve, you'd get an @fsnet.co.uk address and so on.

That worked, but it often gave unwieldly addresses, including full names. A series of third-party webmail providers, not linked to how you connected to the web, began to appear, including Hotmail in July 1996 and its main competitor RocketMail, which launched the same year and was bought by Yahoo a year later for $92 million, where it was rebranded Yahoo Mail. More than 8.5 million people signed up for a free Hotmail account within eighteen months of its launch, each of whom had a massive … two megabytes of storage. It made sense: the service was free, and server storage was costly. But as the internet became increasingly multimedia-led with images and videos, and more people interacted with one another via email, users could quickly find their inboxes overflowing.

Which was why, when combined with the 1 April date on the press release, people didn't believe Google when it announced it was opening up beta access to a free webmail service called Gmail that would give each user 1 gigabyte of storage as standard – 500 times more than Hotmail.

Gmail had been in development since 2001, and it materially changed email forever. You didn't have to delete messages from your inbox. You could even email yourself large files to free up space on your computer, as I did. It was a precursor to the idea of cloud-based storage and is also personally responsible for my own busy Gmail inbox (current unread messages: 314,760), the username for which I snagged shortly after Gmail was announced. The beta tag on the utility, which indicated that it was still being tested and could go wrong, lasted until July 2009.

It can be difficult to imagine now, when Gmail powers the email accounts of big businesses as well as billions of individuals,

An early version of Gmail.

Google takes the Eiffel Tower offline

Occasionally, something happens that demonstrates the sheer might of the internet and its power to tap into the collective consciousness. Usually it involves a rapid and uncomfortable collision between the real world and the online one. And in March 2015, to mark the 126th birthday of Gustave Eiffel's grand triumph, one of those examples of the internet's power happened.

At first it appeared to be relatively innocuous. Google, as it had done for years, decided to devote its 'Google doodle' – the graphic you see above the search bar in place of its logo – to the Parisian landmark. Google's logo was switched out for a piece of art by French visual development artist Floriane Marchix, which, if clicked, took you to the Eiffel Tower's official website.

There was just one problem. Google is used by billions of people every day and, for many, is the front page of the internet. Curiosity caused many of them to click on the doodle, driving vast volumes of internet traffic to the Eiffel Tower's website, which crashed under the pressure. It was an accidental distributed denial of service (DDoS) attack, the type hackers use to deliberately intimidate the owners of websites.

It was some birthday treat for the tower.

but people were reticent at first to use the service. The reason? They groused about the potential connection with the search giant. There was a growing recognition of the power of user data and the breadcrumbs that we give tech giants like Google. Allowing the company to peek into the contents of our emails, along with our stream of consciousness web searches, seemed like a step too far for some.

Little did we know then what would lie ahead.

The first big social platform

In the world of internet-connected, business-literate web browsers in the late 1990s, there was no buzzier topic than the Cluetrain Manifesto. A selection of ninety-five maxims about how the internet would change marketing, its authors said: 'The Internet is enabling conversations among human beings that were simply not possible in the era of mass media.'

They were right, of course – but also slow. Inhabitants of BBSes and Usenet groups had been having conversations for decades. Even the idea of social media was old hat by then: Six Degrees was set up in 1997 by lawyer Andrew Weinreich and is widely considered the first social media platform. Users could set up a profile to show their six degrees of separation from others by posting their friends and family in the form of lists that could be pored through by other users (you could also post on bulletin boards controlled by your top three connections). At its peak, Six Degrees boasted 3.5 million users and was sold in 1999 for $125 million, but it would ultimately become a casualty of the dot-com boom and bust.

Ever a lawyer, and realizing he had something special, Weinreich submitted a patent application as soon as Six Degrees launched for how to develop a social network. The approval process would take four years and came on 16 January 2001.

But just because Weinreich had patented the idea of how to develop a social network, it didn't mean others wouldn't try. One that ventured out onto the web on 1 August 2003 was MySpace.

The front page of Six Degrees.

The site was developed by employees of a Los Angeles marketing firm and became popular because of their marketing nous. Early popular users included a number of music artists, including Arctic Monkeys, who sought to build loyal fanbases by being present on the site.

The person behind the whole shebang was inescapable: Tom Anderson. Users who signed up to MySpace would be asked to select their top eight friends to display on their profile page (which could be customized to look how they wanted and could embed their favourite music). But Anderson never wanted users to feel lonely: as soon as they set up an account, their first friend would be him.

Anderson, known by the site's users as MySpace Tom, would become pretty popular. MySpace became the first social media platform to reach a million monthly active users in 2004. Its popularity was in part thanks to another competitor's misstep on content moderation.

Tila Tequila

In 2003, Tila Tequila was in her early twenties and a sensation on MySpace competitor Friendster. The reason? She was attractive, funny and willing to post risqué photos of herself on her profile. She was decreed one of the first bona fide online celebrities, with people – usually straight men – flocking to her profile to ogle. There was just one problem: Friendster didn't like the images she posted. After the fifth time her profile on Friendster was deleted, causing her to have to rebuild her fanbase, Tequila had had enough.

She brought her 40,000-strong following to MySpace, and the site boomed. It would be bought a year later by News Corporation, Rupert Murdoch's media arm, for $580 million. But Murdoch's entry into the world of social media was a costly error: MySpace was on the wane because of another competing platform on the rise.

The rise of Facebook

The name 'Facebook' now has an intense connection with the idea of oversharing, tedious life updates and likely an unhealthy number of messages or likes from an elderly relative. But for Mark Zuckerberg in September 2001, 'Facebook' was something else.

The teenager was studying at a New Hampshire boarding school at the time and was obsessed with computer coding. At Phillips Exeter Academy, where the entrepreneur studied, the Facebook was a list of every student's name, photograph, address and phone number. The Facebook was an institution, but it wasn't online. However, a schoolmate, Kristopher Tillery, wanted to change that.

He uploaded the Facebook to the internet, allowing any pupil to access another's details with the click of a mouse.

It was a moment Mark Zuckerberg, then seventeen, would never forget. Fast-forward two years to 2003 and Zuckerberg was now studying at Harvard University. He wanted to set up what he saw as a fun website for his male friends to rate their female classmates. The website he produced, FaceMash, split opinion. Those doing the rating loved it, finding it hilarious and an entertaining diversion. Those being rated were understandably less keen.

Several student groups complained to Zuckerberg and to the university, who investigated FaceMash. The site, which attracted 450 people to vote 22,000 times on pictures of their female classmates, was shut down in two days.

Zuckerberg managed to fob off criticism by claiming that his site was little more than a coding exercise that had got out of hand. He never expected the site to become popular. 'This is not how I meant for things to go, and I apologize for any harm done as a result of my neglect to consider how quickly the site would spread and its consequences thereafter,' he wrote to Fuerza Latina and the Association of Black Harvard Women, two groups of students who complained about FaceMash.

Questions remain about the seriousness of Zuckerberg's contrition, even today – questions made all the more pertinent by the fact he pretty quickly dragooned three fellow students, Eduardo Saverin, Dustin Moskovitz and Chris Hughes, into building a new version of the site focused on social networking that learned from the best (and worst) of FaceMash.

The site launched in February 2004. Its name? The Facebook. Zuckerberg had registered the URL that January. At first, the site was limited only to Harvard University students. Its exclusivity and novelty made it quickly grow.

It also set an unusual precedent: people were willing to share their data en masse with the site. The readiness with which people were happy to give their real names, photographs, dates of birth, relationship statuses, interests and even class timetables with The Facebook even puzzled its founder. In an online chat with a friend, Zuckerberg was baffled:

Zuckerberg: i have over 4000 emails, pictures, addresses, sns

Friend: what!? How'd you manage that one?

Zuckerberg: people just submitted it

Zuckerberg: i don't know why

Zuckerberg: they 'trust me'

Zuckerberg: dumb fucks

By June 2004, The Facebook had expanded beyond Harvard, signing up a quarter of a million users across thirty-four different universities. Peter Thiel, the co-founder of PayPal, ploughed $500,000 into the company in August. By the end of 2004, it was a million users strong. The average user logged on four times a day. Those numbers began interesting other investors: in January 2005, the *Washington Post* offered to purchase a stake in the company; Zuckerberg deliberated, then turned them down.

The venerable newspaper was far from the only courter of the company, which renamed itself simply Facebook in 2005. By the end of 2005, it had expanded outside the United States to universities and high schools, taking the userbase to 6 million

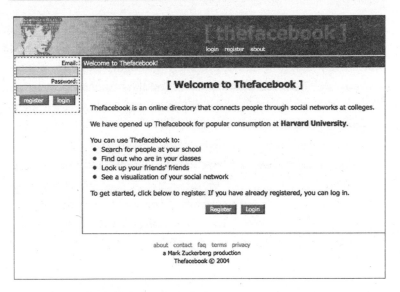

How The Facebook looked in its early days.

monthly active users. In 2006, the site was opened to anyone over the age of thirteen, a policy which remains to this day. Zuckerberg turned down an offer in 2006 from huge Web 1.0 internet giant Yahoo to purchase the company outright for $1 billion.

It proved to be a smart decision. Today, Facebook – which has since been renamed Meta – is worth $490 billion.

The News Feed
One of the ways in which Facebook capitalized on its popularity, and regularly made users come back for more, was a pivotal change made on 5 September 2006. Until then, users had to proactively seek out information about their friends and connections by visiting their profiles. It was the equivalent of heading over to their house, knocking on the door and being let inside for a catch-up.

But that changed with the release of the News Feed. It was

Zuckerberg's big idea to keep users engaged, and it would provide an endless stream of information brought to you, rather than you having to seek it out. It pushed you updates on your friends – changes in their relationship status, updates to their profiles or new photographs they'd uploaded or been tagged in – as opposed to making you pull it down to view.

Zuckerberg, and the broader company, didn't tell its users that what would be the most significant change in how Facebook worked was coming on that September 2006 day. Instead, people were migrated onto it automatically. They saw a brief description of what the News Feed was and then were asked to click a button. It wasn't a 'Yes, I want this' or 'No, I don't' option. It was simply a button reading, 'Awesome'.

Users hated it. Seven in every 100 Facebook users signed up to a single Facebook group set up to oppose the change. Particularly concerning to users was the fact that information they had previously thought was relatively private – within the 'walls' of their own internet fiefdom – was now being broadcast to anyone who they connected with. Within twenty-four hours, Zuckerberg issued an apology – sort of. Titled, 'Calm Down. Breathe. We Hear You.', it sought to reassure users that, actually, nothing had changed about users' privacy settings.

The note, lacking contrition, expressed regret that people felt they had been wronged but told them that, ultimately, the company knew better and wouldn't be changing course. It was a message that would be echoed multiple times over the years. (One of the most recent examples was when users vehemently opposed changes that diluted the appeal of photo-sharing app Instagram, by then owned by Meta, by whacking multiple short-form video features on top. The boss of Instagram released a video saying he understood people were angry, but the company was right to change.)

Facebook's API and Farmville

The same year as Facebook unveiled its News Feed, which would change the way we consume content, it also made a major play for controlling how we interact not just with the site itself but with the wider internet.

Application programming interfaces, or APIs, came about around the same time that the internet was first developed: the term was coined in a 1968 academic paper called 'Data structures and techniques for remote computer graphics' and was expanded on for the internet era in 2000 by computer scientist Roy Fielding. Fielding wrote a dissertation that introduced a way of architecting software that would standardize the way the web worked, making it easier for different services to interact with one another.

APIs are the synapses of the internet, connecting how different elements work together. In Facebook's case, the API was designed as something of a land grab – making it easier for Facebook's millions of users to connect their accounts to third-party services and for third-party services to appear on Facebook with the minimum possible friction.

Computer software developers could, using Facebook's API, create software that users could access through Facebook. In exchange, those software developers gained insights into the users by piggybacking on their Facebook data. You could learn, for instance, what groups the person who used your service and accessed it through Facebook's API was a member of, or who they were friends with on the platform.

APIs had been used by other companies, including photo sharing website Flickr, online auction platform eBay and the everything store, Amazon, for years. Twitter, seen at the time as one of Facebook's main competitors, launched their API alongside Facebook's in 2006, as did Google, utilizing the masses of information it stored about users. But it was Facebook's that would lead the way.

By November 2007, more than 7,000 applications that lived on Facebook and used Facebook's API had been developed, and another 100 were being added every single day. They included quizzes and games, some of which were designed to be useful and some of which were designed to be little more than diversionary.

One of those in the latter column was Farmville, a game designed by San Mateo-based developer Zynga, which launched on Facebook in June 2009. Players were encouraged to tend to crops, gaining experience and points that could be used to build more machinery. They could visit neighbouring farms – owned by their Facebook friends, utilizing the Facebook API – to help them out with ploughing their fields for additional credit.

At its peak in March 2010, 34.5 million people were playing Farmville every single day (around one in every twelve active Facebook users). Tending digital representations of crops became a phenomenon – and one enabled by APIs.

Facebook would go public in February 2012, raising $16 billion from those who wanted to buy stock and consequently giving it a market capitalization of $102.4 billion – nearly fifty-four times larger than Google's market value when it launched its initial public offering in 2004.

Cambridge Analytica

However, APIs caused an issue for Facebook in another situation and another era, and it was one that threatened both the existence and the reputation of the publicly listed company.

A year after Facebook floated on the stock market and when it was riding high, in 2013 a data scientist called Aleksandr Kogan utilized Facebook's API to launch This Is Your Digital Life. Like many of the apps that were built around the Facebook API, This Is Your Digital Life was a quiz that promised, with little evidence, to get deep into your psyche and tell you what you were like. Users answered questions that psychologically profiled them.

Unlike many of the apps built around Facebook's API, users of This Is Your Digital Life weren't giving up that information for free. Around 300,000 users were paid to install the app on their Facebook profile and take the test, giving Kogan's company insights into their lives. It was an academic survey, users were told, where their data would only be used for academic research.

It wasn't just those 300,000 users that the firm ended up collecting data about, however. As well as building up detailed psychological profiles of those paid users, Kogan's app also pulled in the personal data of anyone who was connected to those who took the survey. It turned out 87 million people's data was hoovered up in the process. Importantly, at the time it wasn't illegal under Facebook's terms and conditions to gather data from a user's Facebook friends without permission – a loophole Facebook closed in 2014.

While the data wasn't proactively sourced from a survey and therefore wasn't as detailed, it was still pretty granular. At the time, Facebook allowed you to express interests about everything from types of cheese to favourite TV shows and movies, as well as to join groups of like-minded people across social and political issues.

It was that level of insight that intrigued Kogan and others who had spotted the potential of Facebook ad targeting.

Facebook had built a huge ads business by promising to deliver brand messages to users on an incredibly detailed level. Want to specifically target a middle-aged divorcee with your fashion brand? You could on Facebook. Politicians quickly realized it wasn't just businesses who could benefit: they could too.

A series of revelations

Clearly, the Cambridge Analytica scandal was damaging to Facebook's reputation. But it wasn't the first time Big Tech had faced brickbats.

In June 2013, the *Guardian* and the *Washington Post* published a series of stories based on leaked documents contained within a series of forty-one PowerPoint slides published by Edward Snowden, a former contractor at the National Security Agency.

The revelations uncovered by Snowden showed that the United States gathered information en masse from technology companies including Microsoft, YouTube, Apple, Skype and AOL through a scheme called PRISM, which allowed security agencies to access user data through specially designed 'backdoors' that enabled spies to snoop on internet traffic passing through those services' servers. It blew a hole in the idea that you could use major web-based services without your data being spied on by authorities – and gave rise to the movement of tools that promised end-to-end encryption, such as Signal.

That tackled the problems raised by PRISM, but Snowden's revelations also included 'upstream' wiretaps on undersea internet communications cables, physical

Cambridge Analytica, a consulting firm, worked with Kogan and the data he had gathered. They began touting the dataset around businesses, saying it was a useful addition to Facebook's ad targeting to identify what people were concerned about and aspired to. Cambridge Analytica claimed to have around

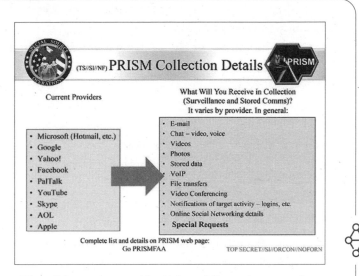

The slides uncovered by Edward Snowden revealing the PRISM programme were a revelation.

intrusions onto cabling that siphon off data, which are trickier to avoid. Shortly after the existence of PRISM was published, the source behind the documents – Snowden – revealed himself in an interview with the news organizations. His US passport was cancelled while he was in Moscow's Sheremetyevo airport, and the whistleblower remains stuck in Russia forevermore.

5,000 data points on each of the hundreds of thousands of people who used This Is Your Digital Life. That level of detail was a gold mine for politicians looking to curry favour with the electorate.

The company ended up supporting Ted Cruz and Donald

Trump in their 2016 presidential campaigns – the latter of whom was, of course, successful.

By March 2018, news of the deliberate targeting of users for political gain based on their psychometric profiles was published by the *Observer* and *The New York Times*. This was thanks to a whistleblower called Christopher Wylie, who used to work for Cambridge Analytica but became disillusioned with what the company had done in allegedly helping to sway the outcome of the 2016 US presidential election. People worldwide were shocked at the power of Facebook to know what they worried about – and how it could theoretically sway their real-life interests.

The company lost 10 per cent of its value as stock traders deserted the firm. Facebook executives, including Mark Zuckerberg, were hauled in front of political inquiries to explain themselves. 'We've been working to understand exactly what happened with Cambridge Analytica and taking steps to make sure this doesn't happen again,' Zuckerberg told a US Senate meeting in April 2018. But even if it never did, the damage was done: Facebook and Cambridge Analytica were forever intertwined in ignominy. One survey, conducted by the Factual Democracy Project in March 2018, found that just one in four Americans held a favourable view of Mark Zuckerberg after the scandal.

Going Meta

While it might be tempting to see Facebook's October 2021 rebranding as Meta as an attempt to shirk the link to the Cambridge Analytica scandal, it's far from the main reason that the company decided to change its name.

Mark Zuckerberg had always thought of his company as more than a simple social network. He believed it could be a tech powerhouse, integral to our lives in a number of different ways.

Indeed, he felt that it could provide some of the key infrastructure that would establish the future of our digital lives, similar to the way the early inventors of the web and the internet helped to shape how we live our lives today.

Zuckerberg believed that with the rise of better, more powerful tech hardware and faster, less lagging internet connections, we would want to live more of our lives digitally. And the coronavirus pandemic, which began in 2020 and saw large parts of the world and our lives unavoidably move relatively seamlessly online, suggested that he wouldn't be pushing against a closed door if he helped us do that.

He anticipated a deeper integration into the digital world in the aftermath of the pandemic and was willing to stake some of his company's fortune and its reputation on it. Zuckerberg thought he foresaw the future and wanted to plant Facebook's flag in this new digital landscape. But he didn't think the Facebook name fit.

In October 2021, Zuckerberg laid out his vision for the future. Facebook the company would become Meta, which would continue to run its suite of apps and platforms but would also leap headlong into developing the metaverse, which we'll explore more in Chapter 6. The metaverse would be a place we'd live, work and play, and the Facebook CEO was so certain we'd love it that he would rename his entire company to show it. Meta was born.

Instagram

As well as better representing the goals of Mark Zuckerberg to develop the metaverse, the name change from Facebook to Meta better represented the scale of the company. Because for the best part of a decade now, Facebook has not really just been Facebook alone.

Today, the company known as Meta publicly reports its userbase across 'the Meta family of apps'. Facebook, the original website and app, has 2 billion users logging on every day and nearly 3 billion every month. But the family of apps can boast 3 billion daily active users and 3.74 billion who use their apps every month.

Two other key apps help boost Meta's user numbers: WhatsApp and Instagram.

Instagram, the photo-sharing app first founded in 2010 by Kevin Systrom and Mike Krieger, was folded into the Meta family of apps through a billion-dollar purchase in April 2012. The deal looked initially like trying to mix water and oil: Facebook, by then eight years old, was starting to lose some of its sheen as its audience aged up. It was no longer the cool college app beloved by students who shared tidbits of gossip and instead was becoming a place where embarrassing uncles overshared about their lives.

Instagram, by contrast, was the cool new thing. It was first developed by Systrom, a former Google employee, as an app called Burbn, where users could check into bars and post photos of what they were drinking. It quickly pivoted name and concept – but kept the centrality of images – and became Instagram, which shunted together the ideas of taking photos using an instant camera and sending them out to the world through telegrams.

Krieger posted the first photo to Instagram on 16 July 2010, from Pier 38 in San Francisco's South Beach Harbour. Four hours later, Systrom posted his own first photo – the app's second ever. Fittingly for the internet, it was a picture of a dog. The app went through months of beta testing before officially being released on the Apple App Store in October 2010. By Christmas, it had a million users. One year later, it had 10 million.

It took until a week before the Facebook acquisition in April 2012 for Instagram to acquire an Android version of the app, but that was no matter to Instagram, which revelled in its exclusive, aspirational aura. Upon buying his latest new toy, Zuckerberg promised to play nicely with it, saying he was 'committed to building and growing Instagram independently'.

That was important to the Instagram co-founders, who wanted to keep the app unique. But, sadly, the promise wouldn't hold up. Advertising was introduced to Instagram in November 2013, a little over eighteen months after it was bought by Facebook. The app was then redesigned a few years later. Users were encouraged to link their Facebook, Instagram and WhatsApp accounts together. By September 2018, both Instagram co-founders were gone. Their parting statements didn't overtly criticize Facebook or Zuckerberg's stifling influence, but readers could fill in the gaps. Systrom and Krieger were 'planning on taking some time off to explore our curiosity and creativity again'.

WhatsApp

Facebook's purchase of WhatsApp was based less on the hunch that a generation was passing Zuckerberg by and more on hard data – acquired from yet another of Facebook's masses of acquisitions. In October 2013, Israeli smartphone analytics company Onavo was the latest company to join the Facebook family. It sat silently on phones and monitored how users opened and dwelt within apps.

Onavo sold up for an estimated $115 million and its leadership joined Facebook. Within weeks, Zuckerberg was asking for Onavo data about how users interacted with WhatsApp.

WhatsApp was launched in early 2009 by two former Yahoo employees, Brian Acton and Jan Koum. The app was initially a way to quickly learn more about the people in your smartphone's address book. Users could update their status to say whether they were at the gym or grabbing a coffee. That all changed in June 2009, when Apple launched push notifications, which proactively tell users about changes in apps they have on their phone. Koum quickly realized those notifications could be used to develop a free, app-based alternative to text messaging. The new WhatsApp was released in August 2009, and users rapidly expanded to a quarter of a million.

By the end of 2013, WhatsApp was huge. It was the world's biggest messenger app, outstripping Facebook's own eponymous service. WhatsApp's 400 million users sent 12.2 billion messages a day, according to Onavo's data – half a billion more than they did on Facebook.

Zuckerberg wanted in on that success. In February 2014, Facebook said it was buying the company – for an astronomical $19 billion. Like Instagram's Systrom and Krieger, WhatsApp's Acton and Koum would also end up leaving Facebook, over a squabble about Facebook wanting to use WhatsApp data to promote targeted advertising to users. In 2017, Acton left the company, later tweeting that people should '#deletefacebook' when the Cambridge Analytica scandal broke.

Koum lasted a little longer, until 2018. When he left the company he had co-founded, he gave an interview to reporters where he summed up what his last few years within the company had been like. 'I sold my users' privacy,' Acton said. 'I made a choice and a compromise. And I live with that every day.'

Twitter

If Facebook was the digital party where we all congregated, then Twitter, as its current owner Elon Musk has identified, is the internet's 'de facto public square'.

But this vital corner of the web's history belies its humble beginnings. It began as a side project to fill one restless engineer's spare time.

In 2005, Jack Dorsey was working for podcasting company

Odeo, which had been founded a year earlier by two former Google employees, Ev Williams and Biz Stone, as well as a third co-founder, Noah Glass. Odeo was a tool podcasters could use to create and publish podcasts and listeners could use to search for them. There was just one problem with Odeo: it was about to be pounded into smithereens by an 800lb gorilla.

Apple announced in 2005 that it would be integrating podcasts into iTunes, its music search and playing software. For Odeo, this was the equivalent of a mom and pop burger joint learning McDonald's is opening up around the corner. Odeo's management knew their time was up and sought to pivot the company. They asked their staff if they had been working on any side projects that could be a lifeboat.

Jack Dorsey piped up: he'd been futzing around with a short messaging service where you could post updates to friends via text messages. It was genius, and pre-dated what would become a vital part of any Facebook user's self-promotional arsenal a year later: the Facebook status update. Because of text messaging limitations, missives were limited to 140 characters.

The Odeo team liked it; Glass suggested calling it Twttr after the sound birds make when chattering to each other. (In the mid-2000s, removing extraneous vowels from tech company brand names was in vogue. Thnk gd tht stppd.)

Twttr was launched on 21 March 2006 as Dorsey posted the first ever message on the platform:

just setting up my twttr

The Odeo co-founders, minus Glass, bought out Odeo and eventually set up a standalone company called Twitter in April 2007. By then, the tool had become the hot new thing in the tech

There's a plane on the Hudson

Chesley 'Sully' Sullenberger had notched up nearly 20,000 flight hours as a pilot in his twenty-nine-year career. On 15 January 2009, Sully was working just another day for US Airways. He was due to hop from LaGuardia airport in New York City to Charlotte, North Carolina, then on to Seattle, Washington, on that day as part of US Airways flight 1549.

Sully never got that far. Shortly after takeoff, at around 3.25 p.m. flight 1549 struck a flock of Canada geese. Both engines shut down, ensnarled with the bodies of the birds. Sully called mayday to the air traffic control tower at LaGuardia, which recommended he turn back and land at LaGuardia. But the pilot quickly realized that wouldn't be possible.

So Sully tried the impossible: landing the plane safely in New York's Hudson River. By 3.31 p.m., the plane had successfully coasted along the river's surface, coming to a slow drift then stop. Passengers used the inflatable slides as life rafts. And someone used their smartphone to post a picture to Twitter.

crowd, thanks to its use being encouraged at that year's South by Southwest festival, held in March 2007.

Twitter was Jack Dorsey's brainchild, and he became the platform's first CEO. In 2009, user numbers increased 1,300 per cent, buoyed in part by Hollywood actor Ashton Kutcher's early advocacy. Kutcher would become the first account to gain a million followers. But it wasn't just Hollywood that helped Twitter become huge. New York did, too.

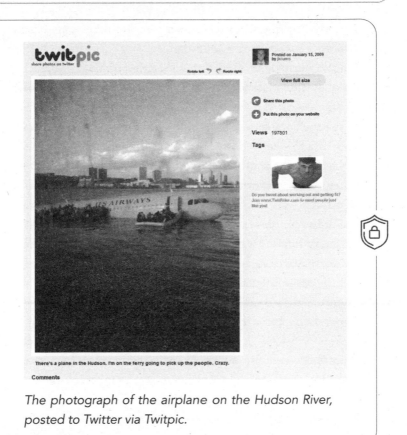

There's a plane in the Hudson. I'm on the ferry going to pick up the people. Crazy.

Comments

The photograph of the airplane on the Hudson River, posted to Twitter via Twitpic.

Breaking news

The Sully landing was the first example of Twitter being used as a breaking news resource. The picture, hosted on third-party tool Twitpic, caused Twitpic to crash as the image spread around Twitter. The site quickly became known as a place to turn when something happened in the world. As an earthquake struck Haiti in 2010, word got out to the world – through Twitter. And as citizens across the Middle East and Africa rose up in opposition to authoritarian rulers in a movement that would quickly become known as the Arab Spring, they spread word of their revolution, once again through Twitter.

And Twitter marked the death of one of the world's worst terrorists, too. In the annals of Twitter history, there have been plenty of memorable moments, but few were as consequential as Sohaib Athar's tweet, posted in the early hours of 2 May 2011. Athar, a software engineer living in Abbottabad, Pakistan, was working on his computer at around 1 a.m., when he heard the unmistakable whir of a helicopter's rotor blades above him.

He did what many people do when they encounter something out of the ordinary: he tweeted it out into the ether. And in doing so, he documented a moment in global history few would forget. It was the mission launched by US Navy SEALs to kill Osama Bin Laden.

Athar didn't know it at the time; he simply posted:

Helicopter hovering above Abbottabad at 1AM (is a rare event)

then follow-up messages as he heard a series of loud bangs. But it would go down in history – and thanks to Twitter, Athar had a curious place in it.

Twitter launched as a publicly traded company in September 2013, worth $31 billion. It introduced an algorithmically dictated timeline in March 2016 (previously, tweets had been presented chronologically). The site doubled the maximum length of tweets from 140 characters to 280 in 2017. Critics feared it would rip the heart out of the site, but it didn't. In fact, Twitter became profitable for the first time in the fourth quarter of 2017.

By that point it had 330 million people logging on every

month and became known as the home of key decision-makers: journalists rubbed digital shoulders with politicians, policy-makers and businesspeople. Including Elon Musk.

Let that sink in: Elon Musk buys Twitter

As we've seen, Twitter helped to propel Donald Trump into the White House in 2016 and to spread right-wing sensibilities around the world. And yet, those most likely to support Trump and share conservative views would often grouse that the platform was biased against them.

The situation was made worse when Trump was banned from Twitter in January 2021, after using the platform to try to incite a revolution to overthrow the rightful winner of the 2020 US presidential election, Joe Biden. Those who supported Trump believed that the ban showed the way Twitter was willing to intervene to silence conservative voices.

Among those who worried about the impact of Twitter's supposed liberal bias was Tesla CEO and SpaceX founder Elon Musk, a South African entrepreneur.

In January 2022, Musk began buying shares in Twitter, eventually, by April, ending up with a 9.1 per cent stake in the firm. It was on 14 April that Musk unveiled his share in the company and launched a hostile takeover bid, saying it was necessary to restore balance to the company for the good of society. The whole project, he said, was founded on the basis of returning free speech to the platform.

Twitter initially fought the takeover before ultimately accepting it – right as Musk decided he didn't want to buy the platform after all. In the summer of 2022, Musk tried to pull out of the deal, while Twitter went to court to compel him to go through with the planned $44 billion acquisition. The case never went to trial;

on 27 October 2022, Musk walked into Twitter's San Francisco headquarters, grinning at a camera recording his entry (he'd later post it to Twitter) while lugging a heavy kitchen sink in his arms.

The imagery was a bad pun. Musk later tweeted:

Entering Twitter HQ – let that sink in!

– a sign to his opponents that things were about to change. He installed himself as CEO, firing the previous executive team.

Things did change, and quickly. Musk fired thousands of Twitter's staff and contractors, resulting in the 8,000-strong workforce being winnowed down to fewer than 2,000. Among those unceremoniously fired were core members of Twitter's content moderation and engineering teams.

The platform struggled to stay online as Musk demanded new features from his skeleton staff, who had lost centuries of collective institutional knowledge about how the platform worked. Glitches, including ones that hampered the ability even to tweet, plagued the platform throughout 2023. Musk promised to step down as CEO of Twitter – once he found someone who he himself said would be 'foolish enough' to take on the poisoned chalice.

At the time of writing in mid-2023, Twitter's past is well documented. Its present is on shaky ground. And its future? That remains unknown. But one significant threat to its future is an app developed by Meta. Threads, launched in July 2023, looks suspiciously like Twitter (now rebranded X)– and managed to nab 100 million of its users within a week, making it the fastest growing app ever.

Reddit launches

The self-styled 'front page of the internet', Reddit is today the tenth most-visited website in the world, with nearly 5 billion visits every

[-] **ComeForthLazarus** 1699 points 2 days ago
Can you explain what your life in Moscow is like?
permalink save report give gold REPLY

    [-] **SuddenlySnowden** `EDWARD SNOWDEN` 2782 points 2 days ago
    Moscow is the biggest city in Europe. A lot of people forget that. Shy of Tokyo, it's the biggest city I've ever lived in. I'd rather be home, but it's a lot like any other major city.
    permalink save parent report give gold REPLY

        [-] **C-4** 3896 points 2 days ago ⊚
        Is winter harsh? Do you ever want to go out, but wake up and find yourself suddenly snowed in?
        permalink save parent report give gold REPLY

            [-] **glenngreenwald** `GLENN GREENWALD` 2502 points 2 days ago
            Canada, Sweden and North Dakota have pretty harsh winters, too. As does Boston.
            permalink save parent report give gold REPLY

                [-] **SuddenlySnowden** `EDWARD SNOWDEN` 5065 points 2 days ago ⊚ x5
                This kills the joke.
                permalink save parent report give gold REPLY

                    [-] **adityapstar** 2828 points 2 days ago*
                    Damn, Edward Snowden is cooler than I thought.
                    EDIT: Did anyone notice what he titled his proof pic on imgur?
                    permalink save parent report give gold REPLY

A screenshot of Reddit, showing the conversation format.

month. But back in 2005, when it was founded, it was its creators' desperate second choice idea after their first failed.

College roommates Steve Huffman and Alexis Ohanian applied to start-up accelerator programme Y Combinator in 2005, with a project called My Mobile Menu. The duo believed their concept could revolutionize how we ordered food by sending orders through mobile text messages. But it didn't woo the funders at Y Combinator.

Instead, the pair came up with the idea for Reddit: an aggregation and discussion platform where people share and comment on links and other multimedia posts they gather from around the internet. The site is divided into subreddits, or discussion groups, based around themes, with many of the most popular ones covering NSFW (not safe for work) topics, including pornography.

The principle behind Reddit was far more sound than My Mobile Menu. It was the thinking person's condensed internet – the newspaper front page summarizing what you needed to know about what was going on online each day. It launched in June 2005.

And again, it flopped. Huffman and Ohanian felt their site looked like a 'ghost town' because of a lack of users, so they created fake profiles and submitted links. Immediately, Huffman would later recall, 'it made the site feel alive'.

Which is a relief: by October 2006, Reddit had become big enough to be bought by Condé Nast Publications, the magazine publisher behind *WIRED* and *GQ*, for more than $10 million. But the site works not because of the investment but because of its community. Reddit moderators – volunteers giving up their time to keep the site tidy and (relatively) abuse-free – collectively do up to $3.4 million of unpaid work each year according to one academic analysis, or around one twenty-fifth of the site's total yearly revenue. Reddit hasn't always got on with its community, most recently, in summer 2023, triggering a site-wide blackout of many popular subreddits unhappy at changes to the site. But it remains a cornerstone of the online experience.

Skype launches

Like many elements of the internet, the history of a key tool that keeps us connected today has its origins in piracy. In 2000, Niklas Zennström and Janus Friis, respectively Swedish and Danish computer programmers, came up with KaZaA, a peer-to-peer file-sharing program in the vein of Napster. Zennström and Friis had lofty ambitions for KaZaA, wanting their platform to be a legitimate competitor in the nascent file-sharing space. But, alas, they were quickly overrun with illicit material that landed them in court. They swiftly pawned off the platform in 2001, to buyers with more of an appetite for court cases, and they used the cash to develop another platform – this time one focused on communication.

Skype was born in August 2003. It used a new technology called voice over internet protocol, or VoIP, which essentially nullified the need for telephones. With Skype, you could call anyone in the world, using the internet, for a far lower price than long-distance calls because you didn't need to use the complicated spider's web of existing phone lines. By October 2003, Skype had 100,000 concurrent users on the service; a year later, that became a million.

That drew the attention of online auction giant eBay, who bought the company in September 2005 for up to $2.6 billion. Even that proved to be a bargain for eBay: Microsoft bought Skype from them in May 2011 for $8.5 billion. By January 2012, Skype was responsible for one in four international calls made worldwide, and by June that year it had 250 million people using it every month. Skype changed the world and laid the foundations for video-calling platforms like Zoom that we use every day, post-pandemic lockdowns. It embodied the internet's twin promises: to make the world smaller and to connect people.

Discord

Skype has increasingly been displaced by other, more niche platforms that have proven popular with younger audiences. If Skype is the online communications tool your parents likely remember fondly from their early days on the internet, Discord is probably the communications tool your children use.

Launched in May 2015 by Jason Citron and Stanislav Vishnevskiy, two veterans of the gaming industry, Discord was designed as a way for ardent gamers to keep in touch with one another while playing video games. Managing to discuss tactics on complicated, team-based games like League of Legends, where you work alongside fellow players to try to beat a team of opponents, was difficult to do. Existing chat and communications apps heavily drained resources, slowing down gameplay, compounding the problem of poor communications and making it more likely your team would lose.

Discord was 'lightweight' – i.e. it didn't require huge processing power on a computer – while being powerful in its features. In January 2016, Discord raised $20 million in funding. Nearly three years later, it raised another $150 million, valuing the company at $2 billion. By 2021, Discord was worth $15 billion and moved beyond the gaming world to be a broader communications platform. Generative AI tools like Midjourney, which we'll come on to in Chapter 6, can run on Discord, and it has a surprisingly broad userbase.

Including Jack Teixeira, a twenty-one-year-old National Guardsman based in Massachusetts, who is accused of leaking numerous classified defence documents from the US military to his friends on the Thug Shaker Central server from late 2022 to early 2023. (Discord communities congregate on servers; some are open to all, while others require you to receive an invite. Thug Shaker Central was of the latter type.) The server was home to between twenty and thirty teenagers and young adults who didn't realize the magnitude of what Teixeira, who used the name 'OG', was doing. While the documents were initially shared only among those users, they quickly found their way onto other servers on Discord, which has more than 150 million users. From there, they found their way onto the broader internet. And Jack Teixeira found himself in custody, charged with the alleged 'unauthorized removal, retention and transmission of classified information that jeopardizes our nation's security'. In June 2023, Teixeira was indicted, and he pleaded not guilty a week later.

Online video

Today, YouTube has become an almost ubiquitous byword for online video. In the same way that we often describe vacuuming our homes as hoovering them or talk about googling a topic on the internet, even if we're not using the search engine developed by Google, so too if you think about consuming video on the internet, you're almost certainly thinking of YouTube's red and white play button.

It wasn't always that way, though.

Before there was YouTube, there were a range of competitors, many of which were set up between the years 2003 and 2005, capitalizing on the rise of higher-speed internet connections that some of the richest and most tech-savvy users were starting to get hooked up to their homes.

A group of Israeli entrepreneurs banded together to launch Metacafe in 2003. At the end of 2004, Vimeo established a platform for independent film-makers, while Grouper bundled together video with photos and music into a single platform. The burgeoning world of online video was even serious enough for its first conference, called Vloggercon, remnants of which are still stored on the Internet Archive, which we'll learn more about in Chapter 5.

Vloggercon took place on the fourth floor of 721 Broadway, New York, home to New York University's Interactive Telecommunications Program, on 22 January 2005. It was a place for video camera-toting hobbyists to gather and talk about the potential of online video – and in that small niche of the internet, word had spread fast. 'Our intimate gathering has become a bit of a spectacle,' said Jay Dedman, one of those behind Vloggercon, before the event.

Indeed it had. Online video was such a sparky world with

potential future importance that Google, which was beginning to become a big beast in the internet world, decided to enter the fray just three days after Vloggercon kicked off.

Its product, Google Video, looked like it would win the race for supremacy in the world of online video. The company behind it had near-limitless resources and at the time was quickly becoming synonymous with everything that was cool on the internet. It had launched Gmail a year earlier; its search engine was far and away the most popular in the world. It was Google's race to lose.

And it did. To a young upstart it would end up buying, called YouTube.

Me at the Zoo: the story of YouTube

The concept behind YouTube was thought up in the early months of 2005 by Chad Hurley (the son-in-law of Jim Clark, who founded a range of Silicon Valley start-ups, including Netscape, which, as we learned in Chapter 2, developed one of the earliest popular web browsers) and some of his friends. Hurley began brainstorming ideas with Jawed Karim, who was working at early internet payments firm PayPal, and Karim's colleague Steve Chen.

The idea was a video-sharing website. On Valentine's Day 2005, the trio came up with a name they thought was ideal: YouTube. It evoked the nickname of the 'boob tube', which some people called television, but was designed for individuals. For You.

In an email sent to Hurley in late February, Karim admitted that he thought the concept for YouTube was a winner. 'I think our timing is perfect,' he wrote. 'Digital video recording just became commonplace last year since this is now supported by most digital cameras.' But it wasn't going to be a place just for videos: Karim had pinpointed another site that did just that, stupidvideos.com, which had flopped.

No, the idea for YouTube was to host videos – but also to find love. 'I believe that a dating-focused video site will draw much more attention than stupidvideos. Why? Because dating and finding girls is what most people who are not married are primarily occupied with,' Karim reasoned. 'There are only so many stupid videos you can watch.' Little did he know then what we know now ...

The site was launched with a single video showing Karim at San Diego Zoo that was posted online on 23 April 2005. YouTube almost didn't happen – when the trio learned that Google had launched Google Video in January 2005, they seriously considered giving up the whole thing.

But they went ahead anyway, and the eighteen-second video of Karim awkwardly talking in front of the elephant enclosure was posted. It would signal a sea change in how we consume content on the internet.

YouTube would quickly become a major destination for people seeking diversions on the World Wide Web. By September 2005, a little over four months after launching, 100,000 video views were recorded every day – causing consternation among those behind the site as they struggled to keep the servers from crashing under the weight of traffic. (The decision in June 2005 to allow YouTube videos to be embedded on other sites also didn't help: users could share videos across the entire web, using up YouTube's bandwidth, without necessarily visiting the site itself.)

Alongside the home movies that people posted were pirated copies of traditional TV programmes, including one skit from comedy sketch show *Saturday Night Live*, called 'Lazy Sunday'.

The two-minute sketch, which saw Andy Samberg and Chris Parnell rap about how they wanted to buy cupcakes and watch *The Chronicles of Narnia*, was first posted online, not on YouTube, but by the TV show in December 2005.

When the sketch appeared on YouTube shortly after, it quickly became one of the most popular videos on the platform. In its first week, it attained 2 million views. Chad Hurley wasn't sure how it got onto his site, so he sent an email to NBC telling them that if they hadn't uploaded it, and they wanted it to be removed, to just tell him. He didn't get a reply until early February 2006, when an NBC lawyer said it needed to be taken down – alongside all the other pirated videos from *Saturday Night Live* that existed on the site.

What had happened was a perfect example of how the internet is bent to the will of its users – always has been, and always will be. Presented with a platform upon which users could store videos, they did what they always will: ignore the rules the platforms put up and post videos, even if they don't own the rights to them. Look on YouTube today and you'll find thousands of copyrighted videos that aren't posted by their rightful owners. It's the same on every platform.

But it became a massive problem for YouTube – because it was a massive problem for Viacom, which owned NBC, where *Saturday Night Live* was broadcast.

The television network sued YouTube, claiming 'Lazy Sunday' was one of at least 150,000 unauthorized clips of copyrighted work hosted on the platform, all of which had been watched 1.5 billion times. 'Some entities, rather than taking the lawful path of building businesses that respect intellectual property rights on the Internet, have sought their fortunes by brazenly exploiting the infringing potential of digital technology,' Viacom wrote in its legal complaint. 'YouTube is one such entity.'

The lawsuit was eventually settled, after YouTube was bought by Google. But copyright problems would continue to blight YouTube.

How online video changed

YouTube went from strength to strength, even if it struggled at times to keep a lid on its copyright issues. The platform started to shift from being a place people posted either copyrighted material featuring celebrities or their shabby home videos, to something in between.

YouTube's online video ecosystem started to evolve into one that was populated by 'creators': people who were trying to professionalize the regular posting of video content created outside the industrialized system of Hollywood studios. 'YouTube in 2006 was people just uploading videos of their pets or very weird comedic sketches they'd shoot with themselves,' said Michael Buckley, who was one of those early creators. 'There was no high-quality content. But there were very high, very personal interactions within the community because there were so few of us.'

There were few creators but many consumers. Traffic to YouTube quadrupled between January and July 2006, when it broke into the top fifty most-visited websites, with 16 million visitors. Every day, 100 million videos were being watched, compared to the 100,000 recorded daily just ten months earlier. One of the most watched videos of the time was a two minute, forty-five second clip of footballer Ronaldinho clowning about while showing off his Nike Tiempo Legend boots.

The shakily shot video was an early example of online guerrilla marketing: uploaded by a poster called Wander Orsi, we were meant to believe this was a totally organic moment. In reality, it was a carefully edited, minutely crafted moment. But it worked: the video became the first ever on YouTube to cross a million views.

By comparison, Google Video was slumping. The tech giant's equivalent of YouTube was struggling to gain an audience and,

Get money, get paid

Creators on YouTube were beginning to recognize the power of money. Brendan Gahan, who was working at an advertising agency in San Francisco, recommended to his bosses that they try advertising a client, an iPod competitor called Zvue, through YouTube.

Two huge names on the site since almost the beginning of YouTube were Anthony Padilla and Ian Hecox. Together, the two were called Smosh, a riotous comedy duo who set up shop on YouTube in 2005. Gahan had seen their popularity – Smosh was the fourth most popular channel on YouTube in September 2006, with what was at the time an eye-watering 17,500 subscribers – and thought they could help influence sales of the Zvue.

So he came to Padilla and Hecox with a proposition: his company would pay the pair $15,000 to mention the Zvue in a video. It didn't have to be a hard sell. It just had to mention the product. In December 2006, Smosh uploaded a short video sketch called 'Feet for Hands', where one character was presented with the audio player halfway through the skit. They got their money. What we now know of as 'influencer marketing' – a $100 billion industry today – was born.

Within a year, YouTube had caught up, first placing video advertisements for products into those posted by users onto the site in August 2007, then launching its Partner Program, which gave creators a share of the income from those ads, in December 2007. The business model around videos on the internet was starting to be built.

more importantly, failing to find relevance against its nimbler competitor.

Rather than trying to beat YouTube, Google decided to join them – literally. On 9 October 2006, Google announced it would buy YouTube for $1.65 billion.

Usually, the purchase of a smaller competitor by a larger company would involve the smaller company moving into the bigger company's hierarchy. But in this instance, Google Video staff members were told to pack up and move to YouTube offices. Google Video was eventually subsumed into YouTube in June 2012.

YouTube under the Google corporate umbrella continued largely on the same trajectory. The same undercurrent of individuals looking to stretch their creative muscles kept posting oddball videos onto the site, which kept attracting new viewers. And with the new viewers came new staff members to keep the quick-growing site going. The site had Google money now and could afford Google levels of staffing.

Broadcast Yourself

Today, YouTube is an online video behemoth. More than 500 hours of video are uploaded to the platform every single minute, with more than 2 billion users. Google, the company behind it, earned $8 billion in advertising revenue from YouTube alone in the last quarter of 2022 – around half of which went to the individual creators posting on the platform.

The site has faced its fair share of issues between being bought by Google and the present day, however. It launched a subscription service in February 2016 – which underwhelmed, in large part because it focused more on celebrity endorsements than on the home-grown stars that made YouTube a must-visit destination. In February 2017, UK newspaper *The Times* reported that YouTube was serving up adverts for holiday resorts and home cleaning products alongside terrorist recruitment videos. The ensuing abandonment of YouTube by its corporate sponsors was called the adpocalypse. Two years later, advertisers fled the site once more after paedophilic comments were found plastered across videos featuring young children.

In spite of all those issues, YouTube has survived and is still going strong. But online video is changing. And that's down to one app.

TikTok

If YouTube, Facebook, Twitter and Instagram quickly grew to a dominant position in the online world, they look like snails in comparison to TikTok. The short-form video-sharing platform has more than a billion users around the world who spend, on average, longer on the app than the length of an average feature film. It grew to that size in around half the time it took its older competitors.

And it has an interesting, controversial backstory.

TikTok is the brainchild of ByteDance, a Chinese tech company first founded in March 2012 by entrepreneur Yiming Zhang. ByteDance developed a suite of apps including one called Toutiao, or Today's Headlines, which presented users – and there were 10 million of them within three months of its launch – with a tailored selection of news stories based upon their interests.

Toutiao, released the same year ByteDance was founded, was powered by an all-seeing algorithm that analyzed user behaviour and presented them with similar content.

The Toutiao algorithm, which focused on text stories, would be useful for ByteDance's next big app: Douyin. Riding high on the success of Toutiao, the company released Douyin in September 2016, piggybacking off the popularity of short-form video apps like

Vine (founded in June 2012 in the United States) and a Chinese competitor called Kwai.

Douyin was developed meticulously: ByteDance analyzed how 100 different short-form video apps presented their content, and picked the best elements from each to put into their own app. The approach worked. Douyin became popular in China and expanded beyond the country's borders in May 2017, was renamed TikTok and split off into its own app with its own development (though in reality, TikTok borrowed many features of Douyin on a several-month delay once they'd proved to be popular in China). A merger of TikTok with a competitor, Musical.ly, was announced in November 2017 and completed in August 2018.

By January 2018, TikTok had around 54 million people using the app every month. By the end of the year, that had grown to more than 270 million. The year after that, it was 507 million. By July 2020, nearly 690 million opened the app regularly – nearly three times as many as Twitter, which was founded a decade earlier.

But it was fortuitous timing, and the pursuit of diversions from the coronavirus pandemic, that truly helped TikTok. In March 2020 alone, users spent as much time on the app combined as there has been between now and the Stone Age. User numbers

TikTok's full-screen, immersive video captures the imagination.

ballooned, and this time more of them were willing to go in front of the camera, too.

TikTok's security risk

In the first half of 2023, a head of steam arose against TikTok. The app had long been viewed with suspicion by some of the most Sinophobic politicians in the US, the UK and Europe, but no smoking gun that it was a deep-state plot had been uncovered.

Nevertheless, in quick succession a number of countries blocked the app, usually only on government devices, but a handful followed in the footsteps of India, which banned TikTok and scores of other apps in June 2020 because of its purported links to China.

The justification for the bans and blocks? Unspecified 'national security risks', for which no country has yet provided evidence. But the whole brouhaha shows how geopolitics and global tech are closely intertwined.

The rise of the creator

Ever since YouTube encouraged users to 'Broadcast Yourself' (its motto for many years), the internet has been trying to get us to share more and more of ourselves online.

It started with Facebook's real-name policy, asking users not to hide behind the pseudonyms that dominated forums and Usenet groups in the early days of the era we now call Web 2.0. But YouTube, and the ability to share home videos with more than your immediate family, gave rise to the ordinary individual creator. The *TIME* magazine person of the year for 2006 was 'You'. Not

YouTube, but the new band of individuals called online creators who were posting to sites like YouTube, Facebook and MySpace.

More children now want to be YouTubers than astronauts according to one 2019 survey, showing how much the site became a demonstration of a career path, rather than just a hobby. The creator – sometimes also called an influencer, a term which was added to Dictionary.com in 2016 – became ascendant: two different terms for people posting content on the internet and being paid to test out services or to sway people to buy products.

But YouTube still required ordinary people to put in a lot of time, effort and money to share themselves online. You needed a digital camera at first – though the rise of smartphones, which put a camera in your pocket, alleviated that need. But to make it big, your videos needed to look professional. You needed proper editing software and good lighting and sound, all of which cost money.

It took the release of the iPhone in 2007 to put a camera in most people's pockets. This is the iPhone 4, from 2010.

TikTok managed to capitalize on higher-quality smartphone cameras by also souping up the standard of video they capture through software. Its editing tools are intuitive, and free. Its short video length – initially between fifteen and sixty seconds but now able to be up to ten minutes long, although in practice they are still normally twenty or thirty seconds – also means people aren't as daunted about recording content as they once were.

That's handy, because the gaping maw of TikTok needs new content to keep viewers satisfied; it turns out short-form video churns through content quickly. But it's a successful model, and one that the old guard of online video (and photos) felt they had to echo.

Instagram Reels and YouTube Shorts

Mark Zuckerberg never likes being second. The rise of TikTok had the entrepreneur concerned: he had previously tried to develop a TikTok killer called Lasso, which was tested in Brazil between 2018 and 2020, with little luck. While Lasso didn't ensnare its audience in the way Zuckerberg wanted, he was still eager to try to compete with TikTok in some way after seeing his apps like Facebook and Instagram lose their userbase in favour of TikTok, which was seen as a trendier app among teenaged users.

So, in late 2019, Instagram launched TikTok-alike Reels on a trial basis in a number of countries, including Brazil, where Lasso had failed. Seeing an opportunity, Facebook pushed Reels into India in July 2020, shortly after the Indian government banned TikTok over a geopolitical argument we'll return to in the next chapter. The rest of the world had to wait until August 2020 to use Reels, which shared plenty of similarities with TikTok.

Around the same time, YouTube had begun to pay attention to the rise of TikTok. In September 2020, it released its own

The creator economy

Vloggers, like those who attended Vloggercon back in January 2005, became creators and influencers – most prefer the former, seeing the latter as tainted by the stench of business – around a year later. Smosh's influencer marketing deal in its 'Feet for Hands' video was a watershed moment, followed up by the first in-video adverts from 1,000 partners, including *The Simpsons Movie*, that rolled out across YouTube in August 2007. The adverts, which took the form of a translucent banner that was laid over the top of the video playing at the time, were seen as relatively unobtrusive, and they netted the creator of the video they intruded on around half of the revenue made.

It was recognition that influencers and creators had clout. And it would continue. Today, the creator economy is worth more than $100 billion. It sustains an entire industry of managers, brand deal brokers, ad specialists and advisers who support the on-screen talent who perform for their audiences of millions across apps like Instagram, YouTube, TikTok and Snapchat.

And it means big business. When advertisers start to throw serious money into a space, they want assurances that their cash will be well spent, that the brand messages they're trying to shill to audiences will be well received and not posted against unsuitable content. The content moderator would become more important than ever.

TikTok clone, called YouTube Shorts. The battle for supremacy in short-form video was on.

All three apps were backed by big money tech companies. ByteDance, the parent company of TikTok, is valued at $220 billion by some estimates, while Google and Meta regularly rank among the most valuable companies in the world. And all three are willing to throw big money at trying to acquire and keep users. The reason? The rise of a parallel economy in the Web 2.0 era, called the creator economy.

Content moderation

One former YouTube staff member, who was around in the very early days of the platform, has told me that the site, when it first launched, had no dedicated content moderation team. There were around a dozen people in the office who would chip in. 'Everyone was casually using YouTube during the day to keep tabs on it, and if you saw something that didn't belong there, you'd pipe up and say: "That doesn't belong there."'

From day one, YouTube was worried about the type of content that existed on the platform – but not perhaps in the way you'd expect. Rather than seeking to keep advertisers happy, they were more focused on users. And so, what informal guidelines there were would be based on what they felt their users would countenance. Content moderation was reactive and a reflection of user interests and habits, rather than a top-down diktat.

The word-of-mouth guidelines wouldn't last long, and written rules were introduced when YouTube hired its first full-time content reviewer, who would pore through videos flagged by the early employees to see if they were appropriate or should be removed.

The standards covered a single page and were written by Micah

Schaffer, who would later go on to become a content moderation expert. It covered all the obvious bases: porn, self-harm, graphic violence and snuff films. YouTube's team had spent time on the internet; they knew its darkest corners. It was described by one former staff member as 'a greatest hits of bad things on the internet'.

That flagged content reviewer sat alongside other higher-ranking employees, who quickly began to discern patterns in the questionable content sent up for review. By mid-2006, YouTube had its first informal hate speech policy. Broadly described, it allowed people to say anything they wanted, no matter how abhorrent, as long as it was articulated in a reasonable manner without slurs.

That may sound strange: why let someone spread a belief in eugenics, as the former YouTube staff member told me could happen, and only stop it if they said a wrong word? The idea was classic Silicon Valley libertarianism: sunlight is the best disinfectant. 'That was the thinking; they're going to be saying this stuff regardless, and they might be living next door to you,' the former employee said. 'You should know about it.' But they didn't realize how 'knowing about it' could change opinions.

The evolution of moderation

That was one of the first major failures of content moderation. But the concept had existed on the internet long before YouTube was even founded. In the year 2000, a Jewish user of an online auction site run by Yahoo searched for Nazi memorabilia to buy in France. The sale of such items was prohibited in the country, and because he could find things to purchase Yahoo was breaking French law. Yahoo had banned the sale of Nazi memorabilia by January 2001.

It was one of the first clear examples of a platform intervening to censor content that was deemed unsuitable – in this case, because of a country's laws. But it would be far from the last.

In the early stages of the internet, bulletin boards and the online communities that coalesced around them could be kept largely in check by a handful of people. They were moderators who volunteered their time to keep the peace among warring, often argumentative, individuals.

And they were argumentative: not for nothing did attorney Mike Godwin coin a phrase in 1990 that has since become an internet staple: the longer a discussion on the internet goes on, the more likely that one or more participants will compare the others to Nazis. Godwin's Law was first tabled in 1990 and entered the Oxford English Dictionary in 2012. Notably, while it is a maxim many online swear by, it was partly disproven by a 2021 academic analysis of nearly 200 million posts on Reddit.

But that huge number – 200 million – gives a sense of why the early concept of volunteer-run, hands-off moderation no longer really works. While Reddit does rely mostly on a cadre of moderators for each of its subreddits, who take responsibility for maintaining the standards in each section of the site, few other platforms do.

Content moderation has become a paid job – not a well-paid one, and one often outsourced to contracted workers employed by a handful of companies that specialize in providing the internet's rubbish disposal workers. And that's down to scale.

As of early 2023, Meta employed more than 40,000 people in what it calls 'safety and security' – which includes content moderation. TikTok has 40,000 of its own checking its content to ensure it adheres to what the company wants on its platform. Twitter fired most of its content moderation teams following Elon Musk's takeover of the company on 27 October 2022, but before then it also had thousands who were monitoring content reported to it.

Those content moderators are often overworked, asked to look at hundreds of pieces of content a day to decide whether it meets the standards platforms require of their users. Those standards have since been written down so there's no confusion over them: Facebook released its first Community Standards guidelines publicly on 24 April 2018, but the rules had been in place for several years by then, and the public had gleaned sight of them thanks to intrepid reporting that saw them leaked to the press.

But even when it's written down in black and white and in painstaking detail, the volume of work moderators are asked to do on a daily basis means there are often false positives or negatives – where guidelines are over or underzealously followed – that slip through the net.

The computer eye above

Most tech platforms these days realize they can't survive the swamp of content with human eyes alone – even when replicated tens of thousands of times – which is why they've started integrating elements of computer expertise into the process. As well as handing the workload to low-paid staff toiling in tough conditions, companies are also outsourcing some elements to computers.

Artificial intelligence, and specifically computer vision, is deployed by many platforms to take a first look at the stream of content posted. It performs a cursory look to see if anything could be wrong, then hands off the work to a human moderator to look in more depth. It doesn't always work – the companies involved often boast of high 90 per cent-plus success rates in catching infringing content, which seems like a high number but in reality still means, at a platform scale, that potentially hundreds of thousands of posts are slipping through the cracks.

Obviously, this is a big problem. Content moderation remains a thorny issue that no platform has got right. Its history is littered with failure: a March 2019 shooting at a mosque in Christchurch, New Zealand, was live-streamed on Facebook by its perpetrator as he killed fifty people. Fewer than 200 people watched it live, and it was taken down twelve minutes after the stream ended. But at least one of those 200 had recorded a copy of it and reposted it online. In the twenty-four hours after the attack, Facebook struggled to keep the video in check: more than 1.5 million versions flooded the site.

That was a problem of scale. But other issues have been a problem of taste and decency.

The 1972 photograph by Associated Press photographer Nick Ut, called 'The Terror of War', is one of the most iconic images in humankind. You'll know it: it's an image of a girl, stripped naked as she flees a napalm attack, screaming in pain. It is uncomfortable to look at, yet we do because it's important to remember the horrors of war.

But in 2016, Facebook decreed no one should see it.

A journalist who included it in a list of photographs that changed war posted his story to Facebook. It was removed. The journalist reposted it. It was removed and he was banned. It was an indication of how impactful social media content moderation guidelines can be – in some instances, literally rewriting our history.

Section 230: When is a platform not a publisher?

The intervening hand of platforms – or more specifically, the executives that run them – has become a hotly debated issue as our politics has become increasingly polarized. It can be argued that Donald Trump was the first major leader of a country to be voted in off the back of the internet. In his successful 2016 campaign to become US president, he used Twitter to bypass the mainstream media's scrutiny of his lightweight political statements and beamed his messages direct to his would-be voters using targeted Facebook adverts.

Trump capitalized on the divisions of our politics, which some argue has been exacerbated by social media. While you might think Trump would be a fan of the web and its social media platforms, he isn't. He and fellow Republicans think social media executives tip the scale through their moderation interventions in favour of their opponents – even when evidence proves the opposite, that social media platforms like Twitter tend to lean rightward.

Whichever way these platforms lean matters, because it goes against their founding principles of being platforms through which posts are passed, rather than publishers who have a particular approach.

Section 230 contains 'the twenty six words that created the internet', according to cybersecurity law professor Jeff Kosseff. It's a bipartisan amendment tacked on to the US Congress' 1996 Communications Decency Act (CDA), which made it illegal to distribute 'obscene or indecent' material through the internet to anyone under the age of eighteen, as well as to harass or threaten people online.

The CDA worried the nascent World Wide Web because of its potential chilling effects – those who ran web hosting services, forums or ISPs, for instance, were concerned that they'd be liable for any infringing content that appeared on sites they hosted or were in charge of. So, Section 230 was added. It would provide an exemption for 'interactive computer service providers', meaning they couldn't be held liable for the behaviour of users on their platforms.

The CDA would last less than a year before the Supreme Court struck it down as unconstitutional because it suppressed adult speech otherwise protected under freedom of expression. But Section 230 remained.

In the twenty-five years since, it has proven to be a saviour for social media sites: they can claim to be merely platforms, simply passing through content their users generate, rather than publishers who would be liable for the content they show.

Big Tech: Too big to fail?

The shield provided by Section 230 matters quite so much because the way we think about the web has changed. At the time Section 230 was being drawn up, the things people were posting on the internet would rarely reach beyond their small, sectioned-off communities. Something posted on a forum would usually only be seen by fellow users on that same forum. Content would rarely escape its carefully drawn perimeter.

But the rise of sites like YouTube and Twitter, and apps like Instagram and TikTok, changed that. Web 2.0 transformed from one which was predominately text-driven to a smorgasbord of multimedia – which is eminently harder to control, check and moderate.

The shift was down to a variety of factors. For one, we got better technology, from the advent of webcams, to digital cameras, to smartphones with professional-quality, built-in cameras in our pockets.

That coincided with a vast increase in the average internet speed, meaning more broadcast-quality content became the norm. Since 1997, average US internet speeds have doubled every four years, according to the Federal Communications Commission. The 5G internet we get through our mobile phones while wandering the world offers average speeds that would be mind-boggling to someone stuck on a 56k home modem connection back in the early 2000s. The average 5G download speed of 100 megabits per second is 1,785 times faster than the 56k connection many people started their journey online with.

All of which means people are consuming more varied content, from a variety of creators, more often. Variety is the spice of life, but when everyone is a content creator, more things can go wrong. From dangerous copycat challenges that lead to injury to people with unpalatable beliefs being able to spread hate speech, giving everyone a microphone and a camera isn't always the boon it's presented as.

The protection offered by Section 230 was welcome news for the executives who got rich off Web 2.0. They've managed to ingratiate themselves – and their platforms – into our daily lives in a way that would seem unimaginable to the pioneers of Web 1.0, who sought to flatten hierarchies. We spend our spare time producing content en masse for those platforms (often for free, or for a tiny share of the profits) – something that would likely baffle those from the previous internet era. And executives are happy to furnish their nests and protect their positions alongside their multi-billion-dollar bank balances.

Big Tech has become too big to fail, impossibly rich, intrinsically woven into the fabric of our society and with the power of the law on its side. But as we'll see shortly, the main players are happy to compete, stealing ground from one another. And while we're focused on the internecine conflict between warring companies, there's a bigger fight to be had online.

Chapter 4
Who Controls the Global Internet?

How many internets do you need?

J. C. R. Licklider was prescient in the way he saw the internet evolving in more than one way. As well as foreseeing the opportunity to build communities and span borders, he could see that choppy waters were ahead. 'If networks are going to be to the future what high seas were to the past, then their control is going to be the focus of international competition,' he wrote in an essay in 1980. Little did he know then quite what that would entail.

The internet remains deeply unequal, even all these decades after it was first invented. The International Telecommunications Union, a branch of the United Nations, estimates that one third of the world still remains offline. In Africa, the majority of people are not connected to the internet; three quarters of those globally defined as 'low income' households are not online.

Many of you reading this will be based in rich, Western, well-developed countries. Your experience of the internet is not the global norm. And it's important to bear that in mind when thinking about the ubiquity of the online world in your life – especially for those in the United States. Though American companies create much of the tech we use and the platforms we spend our time on online, people from the States account for less than one tenth of the global internet population.

And even if you're in a country where internet access is commonplace, it doesn't mean your experience will be the same as someone in a similarly well-connected country.

Three quarters of people in China use the internet. Around the same proportion are online in Italy. Same with Russia, where 88 per cent of the population is online, and Sweden which also shares the same proportion. Yet what internet users in each country see, and how they can converse, is drastically different.

That's because of broader geopolitical problems, and the rights to free speech and expression in each country.

Both China and Russia have seen how the internet can help foment revolution – not least in the way that Twitter and online access helped to stoke the fires of the Arab Spring in 2011, which was live-streamed and tweeted as it spread from one country to another, overthrowing dictators – and decided they want no part of that.

While we like to say the internet is a world without borders and a beacon for freedom, the reality is more complicated – and there are more walls than we'd like.

Splinternets: Russia

The concept of the splinternet – a portmanteau of splitting or splintering and the internet – was first coined by Clyde Wayne Crews, a researcher at the Cato Institute, in 2001. Crews didn't envisage his concept to be a bad thing: he just foresaw the running of a series of 'parallel Internets that would be run as distinct, private, and autonomous universes'. But big governments around the world made those parallel internets deeply divided along lines that suited them, not the users.

At the same time as the US was using its military research budgets to develop the internet in their country, Russia began conceiving of a similar series of computer networks to share expertise in much the same way US universities and military institutions were. The Soviet Union (as it was then known) was, at the time, deep in competition with the United States because of the Cold War. The idea of using a technology developed by their sworn enemy was anathema to the USSR, so they came up with their own.

But it wouldn't come into existence until a lot later than ARPANET. The driving force behind the initiative, a bold director of the Institute of Cybernetics in Kyiv called Viktor Glushkov, kept trying to convince higher-ups throughout the 1960s to adopt the idea of something akin to the internet – a collection of networked computers that could centralize control and speed up the way the Soviet Union worked. It was that last proposal that scuppered the initial plans for a Soviet internet, believes Slava Gerovitch, the author of a treatise on why the Soviet Union ended up not building a nationwide computer network. It became far too complicated a project for the struggling Soviet Union to tackle.

Instead, it took university initiatives to bring the internet – or elements of it – to the Soviet Union. The All-Union Academic Network, or Akademset, was launched in 1978. In a show of unity across divides, it would be connected to ARPANET using a common digital standard but remain independent.

That unique relationship was best typified by the odd friendship struck up between Joel Schatz, a hippie and US army dropout, and Joseph Goldin, a Soviet entrepreneur who was obsessed with the idea of global communications. Schatz travelled from the west coast of the United States to install vital equipment and infrastructure to help build the Soviet internet at the height of the Cold War, when he made friends with Goldin. Both men had a shared vision: if the two superpowers who had long been enemies could just talk to each other, relations might be less strained.

Schatz helped broker the connection between Russia and the United States. (Until the 1983 establishment of the San Francisco–Moscow Teleport, a direct line between the US and the Soviet Union achieved with the help of Schatz and Goldin, those in the Soviet Union wanting to connect to the broader global internet would hop onto it through a hub in Austria.)

Relationships remained cordial even through the dissolution of the Soviet Union and the rise of a new, single Russia. Indeed, even before this, the shift in perception within the Soviet Union, to have fewer suspicions about the wider world, helped enormously to turn the San Francisco–Moscow Teleport first into a commercial endeavour in 1986, and then into the rebranded SovAm (Soviet–American) Teleport in 1990.

SovAm Teleport was the Soviet Union's first ISP and was aided by the dedication of Schatz, who left the Soviet Union in the early 1990s. 'Things were really normalizing,' he told a 2016 documentary about the history of the Russian internet. 'It was a very optimistic time, so there was no reason for us to stay there.' In Schatz's mind, the famed Iron Curtain had dropped – both online and offline. By 1990, Russians were connected to popular Western bulletin boards like FidoNet.

But it wasn't to last.

The Soviet revolution

In 1991, as Boris Yeltsin's overthrow of the old Soviet government took place, and traditional media like the Soviet Union's television stations played *Swan Lake* on repeat, information about the coup was exchanged on the Soviet internet.

Researchers with access to the internet, who were largely focused within the USSR's nuclear industry because of the importance of real-time information exchange, began swapping messages about tanks rolling down their streets. They paraphrased Boris Yeltsin's famous speech atop a tank as he decried the government's desperate, violent response to the coup. It would be a landmark moment – and one that hinted at the problems that would come when another authoritarian grasped power.

But before the arrival of Vladimir Putin in the Kremlin, there was an internet to build. The 1990s marked a massive change for what had now become Russia: business became buoyant, and greed was good. Oligarchs began muscling out academics when it came to control of the internet, and many Soviet programmers ended up emigrating to the United States.

The arrival of the World Wide Web in 1993 was echoed – on a slight delay – in the newly open Russia. The first public website in Russia launched in February 1994: sovam.com was the SovAm Teleport's public face.

The internet was slow to get going in Russia: around 2 per cent of the population had online access by the time 1998 turned into 1999, though this number had doubled as 1999 turned into 2000. The year 2000 was, of course, when Vladimir Putin took over from Boris Yeltsin as Russian president, and the approach Russia took to the rest of the world changed drastically.

What had been a tool used to document meaningful regime change in the early 1990s became, less than a decade later, something to be quashed and quelled. Handily for Putin, most people had never experienced the internet, so they didn't know what they were missing – indeed, in 2002 Russia, which was still feeling the after-effects of decades of lagging behind the West thanks to Soviet rule, a staggering 84 per cent of people had never even used a computer. And many of those who had, often would have encountered them not at home, because PCs were incredibly expensive, but instead at internet cafés.

Internet access was quickly identified as problematic for Putin: while a 1996 Communications Law, put in place by Yeltsin, enshrined a constitutional right to privacy for every Russian citizen, the 2000 Information Security Doctrine enacted by Putin identified the burgeoning internet as a national security concern, and wound back some individual rights to freedom and privacy in the case of national security concerns.

SORM: Russian internet surveillance

But despite the idea from the outside that Russians were allowed to do what they wanted on the internet before Putin arrived, the reality was more complicated. In post-Soviet Russia, the long arm of the KGB and its successor, the FSB (or Federal Security Service of the Russian Federation), was never far away.

Russia has long had one of the most paranoid and pervasive counter-intelligence services in the world. And even if Boris Yeltsin was comparatively happy to encourage free expression and widespread use of the internet, the apparatchiks in the security services were not.

So in 1995 they initiated SORM, or the System for Operative Investigative Activities. It was a process enshrined in law that allowed the FSB to wiretap internet communications, including email contents and every website any citizen accessed. SORM was enabled by requiring Russian ISPs to install hardware that would enable the snoops to … well, snoop.

A 1998 update to SORM, snappily titled SORM-2, expanded the powers of the FSB to look at what users were doing online. In 2000, Russia's technology minister, Leonid Reiman, issued an update to SORM-2, which meant that the FSB no longer needed to provide any justification for why they might want to monitor a citizen's online activity. And in the same year, Vladimir

Putin expanded SORM-2's power even further. One of his first acts in charge was to increase the number of agencies able to request data under SORM, from the FSB alone to another seven bodies, including the police. The digital surveillance state was now built.

Russia's internet today

The original SORM has since been supercharged with subsequent amendments, including one in 2012 that monitored social media activity, and another in 2014 that required ISPs to install more modern equipment that included capabilities for deep packet inspection (DPI). This looks into the entire contents of a packet of data, rather than just a high-level version of it.

The internet is overseen by a branch of the Russian ministry of communications called Roskomnadzor, which dictates what can and can't be seen on the Russian internet. Since 2014, Roskomnadzor has maintained a list of banned websites in Russia, which ostensibly includes those focusing on drug use, child abuse and the promotion of self-harm – but which also includes in their dragnet more innocuous opposition sites. That same year Russia also instituted a 'bloggers' law', which required any site with more than 3,000 page views a day to register with the government.

Mandatory registration isn't just for those who want to post on the internet to a sizeable audience, either. In 2014, Russia significantly tightened its grasp; in a speech that year, Putin called the internet a 'CIA project'.

Alongside the introduction of Roskomnadzor's forbidden list and the bloggers' law, anyone using public Wi-Fi anywhere in Russia – even if they were just hopping onto a fast-food outlet's free Wi-Fi to check their Instagram notifications – must hand over their mobile phone number. A similar rule exists for when you sign up to a home broadband deal: you have to give over your information to the ISP, which in turn can give it to the government.

The approach is one that some academics have called 'networked authoritarianism'. It's a combination of hardware-based surveillance and the implied threat of an iron fist within a velvet glove. It's typically Russian, then – but Putin wanted to go further.

The problem for Putin is that Russia, while having severe censorship (think tank Freedom House says that Russia scores a paltry twenty-three out of 100 in its internet freedom index), still has opposition voices that have long used the internet to grouse about the dictator's leadership. Alexei Navalny, the figurehead of the opposition movement to Putin, has frequently used online documentaries to highlight the corruption he alleges is endemic within Putin's government – gaining enormous audiences for his claims.

That causes Putin issues. He's widely believed to have orchestrated an attempted poisoning of Navalny in August 2020 that wasn't successful, and has taken steps to try to exert *more* control over the internet in Russia, in large part by following in the footsteps of another authoritarian country: China.

The Great Firewalls of the world

The history of the internet and its deep rooting in the US military defence space understandably gave some countries second thoughts when thinking about whether to adopt the new technology wholeheartedly. What the internet offered its users – unfettered access to the world's information in an instant, and the ability to contact and converse with like-minded people – was also problematic as a concept for more authoritarian regimes, used to having control over public discourse.

For China, as we'll shortly see, the fact that the country's political make-up was already firmly entrenched to provide absolute control for its leader meant that it didn't have to worry too much about the internet. By the time the promise and potential of a life lived online arrived for the world, China already had control over its people and decided simply to implement – from the beginning – an internet in its own image, where it had the power. Expression was limited and deferent to the ruling party, completely different to the free-for-all we in the West understand the internet to be.

Russia was more complicated. At the time the internet was becoming commonplace thanks to the spread of the web, the centralized control system that had been ubiquitous in Soviet times was crumbling. Its 1990s president, Boris Yeltsin, was happy to see the liberalization of the country. All of which meant that when former KGB man Vladimir Putin got into power at the turn of the millennium, he had to try to put a part-escaped genie back in the bottle.

We've seen in part how Putin tried to do that, but our story only took us up to the mid-2010s. Fast-forward to 2019, and one of the most significant changes Russia could make to its internet was put forward by the president.

In May 2019, Putin announced RuNet, a sovereign internet disconnected from the rest of the world. It was one part of a broader domestic internet law that came into force in November 2019.

The principle behind RuNet involved three key elements: first, packet-snooping hardware would be installed on company networks to further enable the state to check what was being said online by users. Authorities were also given power to centralize control of the internet, while the third factor created a national Domain Name System (DNS) that would mean Russia could ensure no one within its borders can easily access banned websites (Russia is believed to have only ten public internet exchange points where the country connects to the broader online world).

That DNS was the key element of the bigger plan for RuNet: Russia would essentially keep a copy of the global internet, which it could control and through which it could dictate what users would and wouldn't be given access to within its own borders. But maintaining a modified backup of the internet through which to route the traffic of millions of people – seven in every eight Russians are now online, a world away from the early days of the internet there – is hard. On 24 December 2019, Russia claimed it had successfully tested uncoupling itself from the global internet, and no longer needed to be connected to the rest of the world.

The announcement, which was only a test, was greeted with horror by the free world. It was a signal that Russia was turning its back on the rest of the planet and caused consternation about the rise of the splinternet, or the Balkanization of the digital sphere, where everyone breaks off into their own world and no one interacts.

The RuNet test allowed Russia to feel more confident banning access to different websites, which the state felt emboldened to do to quell dissent after its early 2022 invasion of Ukraine. In late February and early March, Russia blocked access to Twitter because of fears it was being used to spread anti-war sentiment.

Russian internet users' responses to the country's invasion of Ukraine, including organizing protests and sharing footage of physical pickets on the streets of Russian cities, further pushed the country to crack down on free expression. Within six months of Russian boots hitting the ground in Ukraine, state regulator Roskomnadzor had blocked access to 138,000 websites, including Facebook, Twitter and Instagram. Others stopped serving the Russian market: in early March 2022, TikTok stopped allowing the uploading of new content on its app within Russia.

The clamp down on websites was an attempt by Russia to

retreat into its own world. 'The whole thing is about control of information,' Alena Epifanova, a research fellow at the German Council on Foreign Relations, a foreign policy non-profit, who has studied Russia's internet censorship and infrastructure, told me. 'They fear information.'

With each step, Russia risks becoming more like China – though the country's leader would likely see that as a good thing.

Splinternets: China

One of the things you quickly learn about the history of the internet is that every key moment is usually mired in failure. Just as the first message sent between two academic institutions in 1969 glitched and crashed out of existence before fully working, so the birth of the Chinese internet had a similarly calamitous start.

It was 14 September 1987 and a team of German scientists had landed in Beijing to mark a key moment for China. Werner Zorn had helped bring his home country of West Germany onto the internet and saw an opportunity to do the same for China. He had embarked on a project to build a supercomputer, part-funded by the World Bank, designed to try to bridge what was seen as a twenty-year gap between the West and China's tech advancements. (Little did we know then that the supposed tech backwater would quickly overtake the West.)

Zorn had worked with a Chinese counterpart, Wang Yunfeng, to connect China to the global internet. And an email sent by Wang on that September day in 1987 would mark China's arrival online.

'Across the Great Wall, we can reach every corner in the world,' wrote Wang in English (the supercomputer could only receive German or English inputs at the time). 'This is the first

ELECTRONIC MAIL supposed to be sent from China into the international scientific networks via computer interconnection.'

There was just one problem: due to a variety of glitches, it took six days to deliver. Still, China was connected to the internet. But unlike the newly opened-up Russia, which was keen to embrace capitalism and the promise of the internet, Chinese authorities remained reticent.

China leveraged American expertise to build its internet, but in its own way. In the 1990s, American telecom company Sprint helped build ChinaNet, the first Chinese internet network outside of the education system. But Sprint ended up getting too greedy, and was muscled out of China's internet infrastructure in the mid-1990s.

By 1994, when Russia was getting fully onto the web, just 2,000 people in China's 1.2 billion population were online: a rounding error. In part, that's because Chinese leaders were not ignorant. They saw the promise of the internet and what it was doing in Russia, and they wanted no part of that revolution. The Tiananmen Square protest, a six-week, student-led rebellion against the Chinese way of governance, happened less than two years after that first email was sent from China, and it served as a warning sign for the ruling Communist Party. The internet was a place to be tamed, they thought; if more people had had access to the internet back then, the protests could quickly have spread.

Chinese premier Li Peng moved quickly in the 1990s to ensure that wouldn't happen on his watch. On 1 February 1996, China's leader signed off State Council Order 195, entitled 'Temporary regulations governing computer information networks and the internet'. It would in fact consign China to travel a totally different path to much of the rest of the world when it came to embracing the web. It allowed, a year later in 1997, the country's Ministry for Public Security to enact laws around the internet that were primarily designed to prohibit the use of the internet as a tool for 'inciting to overthrow the government or the socialist system'.

And in case China's people couldn't be trusted to do that themselves, the state would help, with a massed regime of censorship that's now estimated to cost $20 billion a year to maintain.

Censorship in China

China's Great Firewall – a phrase first used by *WIRED* magazine to describe the country's massive state censorship of the internet – encircles the country's cyberspace. It acts as a fortification designed to prevent any information deemed to be unpatriotic or against the Chinese state's goals from entering the country. That means today in China you won't find much, if any, Western reporting on Tiananmen Square. You won't find much, if any, reporting on the massacre of Uyghur Muslims in Xinjang province. And websites or search engines that help to direct you to that information are stopped on the way in: they can't even get a toe in the door.

The firewall works simply by snooping on all the data coming into and out of the country. This data is parcelled up in packets, and as each one passes through the physical connection points that link China to the global internet (there are surprisingly few: you can count the points where most of the data destined for China passes through on one hand), it's put through a scan.

Think of it like airport security: websites and data are your carry-on luggage. Each one goes through the scan to examine the contents within – and if it's prohibited, it's not allowed through. In reality, it means that a site simply won't connect if a Chinese web user tries to direct their browser to it. Type Wikipedia.org (which has been blocked in mainland China since April 2019) into a browser in China and it'll throw up an error message without explaining why.

But for anything within the country's online castle, or any interloper who manages somehow to find a crack in the firewall and break in, China's internet infrastructure apparatus also works to aid the state. ISPs and companies – including social media platforms and websites operating in China – also adhere to the rules that keep the socialist system in place.

Then US president Bill Clinton thought that such a strong chokehold on something as sprawling as the internet would never work. 'There's no question China has been trying to crack down on the internet,' he told a Washington DC conclave in 2000. 'Good luck,' he laughed. 'That's sort of like trying to nail jello to the wall.'

Yet that's just what China has managed to do: something most others thought impossible. Still, some jello has slipped off and bounced free.

Cat and mouse censorship

Since 1997, Chinese dissident Li Hongkuan has been trying to wriggle his way through the Great Firewall.

Li, who turned sixty in 2023, took part in the Tiananmen Square protests in 1989 and has long thought that the way China is run is dangerous. His way of subverting China's great internet censorship tools is one that we've already encountered before: email spam.

Li managed to build up a huge database of email addresses, running into the hundreds of thousands at a time when the Chinese internet was still being used by less than 2 million, which he put to work in 1997 when he launched Da Cankao (translated into English as 'VIP Reference'). It's a collection of articles that would never be shared within official Chinese state media because they reflect badly on the state or show life outside China in a positive light, which are collated and shared via email.

The dissident deliberately chose to spam users because, he reckoned, there was safety in scale. If anyone got caught with a copy of Da Cankao in their inbox, they could claim they hadn't sought it out; it had come to them, unprompted.

More blatant was the arrival of Western search engines like Yahoo and Google, which arrived in China in September 1999 and September 2000 respectively. It looked like a sensible, obvious choice for the companies: by July 2001, China had 25 million internet users.

While Yahoo struggled to compete against Chinese competitors, Google raced ahead, cornering around a quarter of the Chinese search market by 2002. But success wouldn't last: the site was blocked later that year before being banned outright in 2003. In that time, Baidu, a homegrown competitor, managed to build up its name.

Western tech giants always made uncomfortable bedfellows with the Chinese state. The reason? The requirement for tech companies operating in China to sign the Public Pledge on Self-Discipline for the Chinese Internet Industry, which was tabled in 2002. It required tech companies operating in China to proactively 'monitor the information publicised by users on websites according to law and remove the harmful information promptly'.

It made things uncomfortable for Western tech companies, who cleaved eagerly to a libertarian ideal. By 2005, Yahoo had sold its Chinese subsidiary to a former English teacher called Jack Ma, who had since 1999 been running an e-commerce company called Alibaba that quickly became a conglomerate. In January 2006, Google withdrew its Google.com search engine in China and replaced it with a country-specific one, Google.cn, which kowtowed to the state's demands for censorship. It was too little, too late, however. Baidu had, by 2006, cornered more than 50 per cent of the market.

But Google staggered on in China. It persisted in trying to present YouTube to Chinese audiences but was regularly taken offline or blocked. In March 2009, YouTube was banned totally because it had been used by activists to share videos of police brutality in Tibet. In December 2009, the company realized that Chinese hackers, likely working for the government, had broken into its servers and tracked people viewed as enemies of the state for more than a year, rifling through their Gmail accounts and building up a picture of dissident networks.

Enough was enough. On 12 January 2010, Google announced it would stop censoring search results. The Chinese state stepped in, throttling access to the site and stopping people seeing search results the government didn't agree with. Google had been nobbled – and despite thinking about returning to China in the late 2010s, has largely petered out.

Accessing the internet illicitly

Unable to trust that Western companies arriving in China would not compromise their ideals to comply with local rules, Chinese internet users seeking the truth and wanting more than the curated collection of stories put together by Da Cankao had to go elsewhere. They needed to virtually bust out of the Great Firewall then sneak back in – undetected.

Several tools could help. In 2001, a Chinese-born, US-based Falun Gong follower called Bill Xia, along with several other like-minded people, adapted a tool called FreeNet, which allowed users to host content on the dark web, to work for Chinese users. (Followers of the Falun Gong spiritual movement are seen as a thorn in the side of China because they don't stick to the script the Communist Party wants to present about the country.) FreeNet China was launched in 2001 and spread to several thousand users through surreptitious swaps of floppy disks, on which it could be stored. But Xia and others wanted to make a tool of their own: DynaWeb arrived in 2002, collating vast lists of proxy servers through which Chinese citizens could connect to the wider web.

Proxy servers are simple tools: think of them like hiding forbidden material inside an innocuous book. To someone watching on, it looks like you have a copy of the latest blockbuster book, but buried within its pages is documentation on how to overthrow a government. Proxy servers would act as go-betweens, taking a request from a China-based user to visit a banned website, visiting the website and passing over the information on it, all without the censors knowing. DynaWeb was augmented by competitors including FreeGate and UltraSurf, all of which were designed to sidestep Chinese checks on internet traffic.

Proxies acted as the precursor to virtual private networks (VPNs), which operate in a similar manner and are more commonly used in China these days. (VPNs are also used by plenty of users in non-surveilled states to, for instance, get access to movies or shows that are available on a different country's version of Netflix.)

The Chinese internet today

No better example of the splinternet writ large can be seen than through the Chinese internet, which runs in parallel with, but completely alien to, the Western one most of us know. The traditional names, sites and apps we use simply don't exist in China – but homegrown facsimiles of them do. And it's no longer the case that it's only China copying us: as seen previously, TikTok is a copycat of a Chinese app, Douyin.

TikTok's rise has some right-wing anti-China hawks in the United States, the UK and Europe worried. But the reality is that a single app is unlikely to be a Trojan horse for a wider Chinese attempt to overthrow the internet's hegemony.

The fight for the future of the internet looks likely to end in a stalemate: the Chinese state is unwilling to countenance Western apps coming in and bringing the promise of freedom in the same way that the arrival of pop music, Levi's jeans and McDonald's did to the Soviet Union in the 1980s. You only need to look at a speech current Chinese president Xi Jinping made to the National Propaganda and Ideology Work Conference in August 2013 for evidence of China's unwillingness to budge on that:

> Western anti-China forces have constantly and vainly tried to exploit the internet to topple China … Whether we can stand our ground and win this battle over the internet has a direct bearing on our country's ideological and political security.

And on the other side, the collective governments of the West are unwilling to allow household names on the Chinese internet to get too comfortable for much the same reason.

Free countries also have qualms with the continued existence of the highly censored Chinese internet – in part because it resigns China's population to a life under the thumb but also because its existence encourages other countries to follow in its footsteps, spreading authoritarianism and censorship.

It's of particular concern for the West given the already strong links between China and the continent with the largest untapped resource of unconnected, would-be internet users: Africa. China's soft-power approach, funding infrastructure projects in key African countries as well as providing expertise direct from Beijing, threatens to shape the internet there in a more controlled, less democratic way than the one most of you reading this book are used to – and that could tilt the perception of what the internet is for, and how it's run.

The fight for the future

That battle for the future of the internet is one that those most closely intertwined with its past, present and future know all too well. Just as J. C. R. Licklider compared control of the internet to control of the high seas, so today's totemic figures in the internet space recognize the stakes involved.

In July 2019, Mark Zuckerberg held multiple meetings with his employees at Facebook (which later became Meta). The meetings were designed to allow staff to quiz the chief executive about what his vision for the future was – and to raise their concerns. In one of those meetings, a staff member asked Zuckerberg whether he was concerned about the rise of TikTok.

Zuckerberg's answer was both telling and indicative of the broader battle for the future of the internet being waged not just by regulators and politicians, but by Silicon Valley tech executives who have grown accustomed to being in control.

I mean, TikTok is doing well. One of the things that's especially notable about TikTok is, for a while, the internet landscape was kind of a bunch of internet companies that were primarily American companies. And then there was this parallel universe of Chinese companies that pretty much only were offering their services in China. And we had Tencent who was trying to spread some of their services into Southeast Asia. Alibaba has spread a bunch of their payment services to Southeast Asia.

Broadly, in terms of global expansion, that had been pretty limited, and TikTok, which is built by this company Beijing ByteDance, is really the first consumer internet product built by one of the Chinese tech giants that is doing quite well around the world.

TikTok's globetrotting prowess hasn't escaped the eyes of politicians worried about Chinese influence, either. A year after Zuckerberg was facing questions from his staff, India banned the app alongside several dozen others over a border squabble with China.

It wasn't the last time that the internet and geopolitical concerns would collide. A year later, Donald Trump made TikTok his primary opponent in the 2020 US presidential election, making a pledge to ban the app a cornerstone of his campaign. It didn't work on either front: Trump lost the election, then his administration lost the court case lodged by TikTok to prevent its elimination.

Nor has the fighting stopped. TikTok is still seen by some as a vassal of the Chinese state, a Trojan horse sent to lure us all in with funny videos, then with the flick of a switch turn us all into Little Red Book-quoting foot soldiers for the Chinese Communist Party. Concerns around the integrity of user data led to the European Commission, the United States and Canada banning it from government devices in early 2023.

At the time of writing, the UK had just followed a similar path, banning TikTok from government devices. A bipartisan group of US politicians wants to go further, banning the app from all phones, not just those of government employees. It's clear, through the lens of TikTok, that the future of the internet remains contested.

Chapter 5
How Web 2.0 and the Internet Have Shaped Us

Online shopping

Jeff Bezos was a bored investment banker before he set up Amazon in July 1994. Bezos, who was a vice-president at Wall Street investment manager D. E. Shaw & Co., decided to cross the country to Seattle, Washington, for a fresh start. Despite considering calling his site MakeItSo.com, after the catchphrase used by a favourite TV character of Bezos's, *Star Trek*'s Jean-Luc Picard, the entrepreneur settled on a different name. But it's not the one we're all familiar with today.

Cadabra Inc., as the company was first called, was set up and run out of Bezos's rented home. The name changed when people misheard Bezos and thought he was selling cadavers. Bezos eventually settled on 'Amazon' because the scale of the grand river matched his ambitions for the company.

Another thing that changed? What Bezos wanted to sell. When establishing the firm, the investment banker toyed with selling five popular products: books, videos, CDs and computer hardware and software. But it was books Bezos decided on – taking a year to firm up the business. (It's worth saying that some early employees dispute this founding myth, believing Bezos had always wanted to build a book-based business. It was why, they say, he picked

Welcome to Amazon.com Books!

One million titles, consistently low prices.

(If you explore just one thing, make it our personal notification service. We think it's very cool!)

SPOTLIGHT! -- AUGUST 16TH

These are the books we love, offered at Amazon.com low prices. The spotlight moves **EVERY** day so please come often.

ONE MILLION TITLES

Search Amazon.com's million title catalog by author, subject, title, keyword, and more... Or take a look at the books we recommend in over 20 categories... Check out our customer reviews and the award winners from the Hugo and Nebula to the Pulitzer and Nobel... and bestsellers are 30% off the publishers list...

EYES & EDITORS, A PERSONAL NOTIFICATION SERVICE

Like to know when that book you want comes out in paperback or when your favorite author releases a new title? Eyes, our tireless, automated search agent, will send you mail. Meanwhile, our human editors are busy previewing galleys and reading advance reviews. They can let you know when especially wonderful works are published in particular genres or subject areas. Come in, meet Eyes, and have it all explained.

YOUR ACCOUNT

Check the status of your orders or change the email address and password you have on file with us. Please note that you **do not** need an account to use the store. The first time you place an order, you will be given the opportunity to create an account.

A screenshot of the Amazon home page from August 1995.

Seattle to base his company: there were large warehouses and book companies nearby.)

Amazon opened its doors online on 16 July 1995, according to the company, but a beta test with a select few tech-trendsetters had been running for a few months beforehand. The first book sold was Douglas Hofstadter's *Fluid Concepts and Creative Analogies: Computer Models of the Fundamental Mechanisms of Thought*, on 3 April 1995 to John Wainwright, a famous computer scientist who lived at the time at 215 Alexander Avenue in Los Gatos, California. The first used book? *Fisher's Hornpipe* by Todd McEwen, which was delivered by hand to its buyer – a roommate of Glenn Fleishman, an early Amazon employee turned journalist, editor and author. (Full disclosure: Fleishman read a draft of this book for accuracy.)

Bezos represented a new, trendy shift in society: the dot-com entrepreneur who has a single, trademark wardrobe staple (Bezos's was simple blue shirts, which hung in his office) and mythologizes their humble beginnings (Amazon's great founding gimmick, which is true, is that the company set up employees on desks made of household doors mounted on four-by-four batons of timber).

As for John Wainwright? He had his own impact on the online shopping company: one of the company's buildings is still named Wainwright today, in thanks to the keen shopper. Another name that you'll see a lot on Amazon's campuses is Rufus. It was the name of a corgi who belonged to two early employees, Susan and Doug Benson. Rufus was beloved for his stupidity.

It's no secret that Amazon today is a trillion-dollar company that sells far more than books. It runs grocery stores and has trialled running hairdressing salons. It runs Amazon Web Services, which provides cloud storage and hosting to some of the world's biggest enterprises – including plenty that you log on to every single day. It employs more than 1.5 million people worldwide. It's a far cry from the first week of sales for Amazon way back in April 1995, which totalled $12,438. In its 2022 edition of Prime Day, its annual sales extravaganza, Amazon made that amount of sales in around 0.2 seconds.

What Bezos saw back in 1994 and 1995 was the promise of what online shopping has become today. In the UK, between one in every £4 and one in every £5 is spent online, according to the Office for National Statistics. In the US, it's approaching 15 per cent. Both were accelerated significantly by the pandemic, but the convenience of 24/7 shopping, speedy delivery and simple returns means more and more of us are buying online.

Making payments

But to buy things, you need to have a way of making payments online. The first 'online' shopper bought her purchases before the web even existed – indeed, before most people had even connected to the internet. Even odder, she wasn't the young, computer-literate academic researcher you'd expect to fit the bill.

The first online shop

Jane Snowball was a seventy-two-year-old grandmother living in Gateshead, England, when she bought a tub of margarine, a packet of cornflakes and some eggs in May 1984. The purchase was brokered through the internet, but Snowball didn't have a computer. She used a small bit of hardware that connected to her television called Videotex. It effectively turned her TV into a computer terminal, showing her a list of more than 1,000 groceries she could purchase from her local Tesco supermarket.

Snowball was the guinea pig for the Gateshead Shopping Experiment, which would become online shopping, because she had recently broken her hip and was housebound. Buying items without having to leave her home made sense for her. She paid the driver at the door, because at the time the ability to process payments through the internet was not common.

That would change, though. Pizza Hut claims ownership of the first physical item ever purchased over the internet, a year before Amazon made its first sale, in 1994. The pizza was bought through PizzaNet, the company's online ordering platform, and was a large pepperoni and mushroom pizza with extra cheese.

But those early online purchases were difficult to do, with many early web users worried about handing over their credit card details online. Netscape, the creators of the Navigator web browser, tried to allay fears, developing a protocol or set of rules to process data that would ensure financial information couldn't be snooped on. SSL, the Secure Sockets Layer, was the invention of Egyptian cryptographer Taher Elgamal in 1995. SSL was superseded by TLS, which we've met earlier in this book.

A handful of specialist payment processors were founded around the same time, including GlobalCollect, Authorize.net and Bibit. But invariably they still directly tethered online purchases to bank accounts – which some were wary of. It would take the invention of a more secure technology that would later become known as PayPal to kick-start online shopping in earnest.

PayPal was a product before it was a company. It was run by Confinity, a security start-up set up by Peter Thiel, Max Levchin and Luke Nosek, who have since become known as part of the PayPal Mafia, in December 1998. Confinity initially produced tools that could secure PDAs, or Personal Digital Assistants, and other handheld devices, but the business wasn't working so they pivoted to creating a digital wallet you could use to pay for items online, called PayPal.

At the same time, South African entrepreneur Elon Musk and a handful of his peers launched X.com, an online bank. By March 2000, the two had merged, seeing their strength was compounded by coming together.

PayPal the company was born, and Musk was its CEO. The company soon became interlinked with online shopping sites and was sold in October 2002 to eBay, an online auction site set up by Pierre Omidyar in September 1995, for $1.5 billion. For many people, eBay *was* online shopping.

Despite no one coming to the site on its first day of operation, word quickly spread. Its founder decided to dedicate himself full-time to the site in the summer of 1996, when eBay was making $10,000 a month in revenue. By that autumn, nearly 1,000 auctions were held every day on eBay. PayPal's ease of payments – and the knowledge that any cash in a PayPal account could, in theory, be siloed away from your bank account – helped to boost the online retail economy.

The death of the high street and the gig economy

The history of the internet – and online shopping's role in it – is intertwined with the twinned fate of the high street, or 'physical retail'. Nearly fifty stores a day close in the UK, thanks to lower footfall. People still prefer overall to shop in-store, with 41 per cent of Americans saying they prefer the physical experience compared to 29 per cent who favour online shopping, but it's undoubtedly more convenient to order whatever we like and see it arrive at our door.

The people who bring us our online shopping – whether groceries or other items – are often low-paid workers employed in what's called the gig economy. (Other gig economy workers include the people who deliver your online takeaway order or the Uber drivers who take you home at night.)

Delivery drivers, often driving vans emblazoned with the names of companies like Amazon, shuttle around our cities and roar down our roads. Online shopping has had a real-world impact on traffic: the distance covered by vans measured as a percentage change is skyrocketing compared to cars and other forms of transport. Some cities have seen significant changes to their traffic patterns because of online shopping and are trying to tackle the scourge of online delivery drivers by blocking them from city centres.

The same is true of those who handle packages and letters. While companies like Amazon have their own fleet of delivery drivers, national mail services will often deliver online shopping from other companies. Between 2010 and 2020, the number of letters the United States Postal Service handled every year dropped 30 per cent, from 169.2 billion to 121.8 billion letters. At the same time, the number of parcels it delivered rose from 1.4 billion a year to 7.3 billion.

Online shopping is one of those tangible ways that the internet has changed our physical world – and some would say for the better.

The digital divide

Many key services – from paying money into and taking cash out of banks, to signing up for passports and government services – now happen online. That's convenient when it works and if you have a reliable internet connection or are comfortable using the technology.

But not everyone wants to take part in the relentless march of technology. The digital divide is the growing gulf between those who can or want to take large parts of their lives online, and those who don't.

Though classified as a single split, the digital divide is actually a series of large cracks, like when a sharp object splits through a sheet of ice and creates thousands of individual parts. At a broad level, the divide includes those who live their lives through their smartphones or laptops, and those who don't. That choice is common (but not always an option) in the rich, developed world, but in more developing areas the divide is more obviously split among those who can afford to own a smartphone and have reliable internet connection, and those who can't.

Worldwide, 3.2 billion people live in areas that have access to mobile broadband networks but don't subscribe to a mobile broadband service, according to the GSMA, a mobile phone industry body. That means four in ten people are on the wrong side of the digital divide.

Even having a smartphone isn't a given in this day and age. My parents don't have a smartphone: instead, they've chosen to stick with what's called in the industry their 'feature phones', or non-smartphones, which can call, text and browse the internet without images, on websites designed especially for mobiles. They're not alone – the GSMA says around a quarter of the world's population don't have one either. The proportions vary by where you are in the world: in North America, smartphone adoption stands at 82 per cent. In China, it's 77 per cent. In sub-Saharan Africa, it's just 64 per cent.

My parents' lack of a smartphone means that the links their dental practice sends them via text message, to complete an online form before their appointment, don't work; the QR codes on their restaurant table to order and pay via app aren't accessible; and the better savings accounts interest rates offered by banks to their mobile banking customers aren't available to them.

That's annoying enough, but remember: the rise of online shopping and the move to an app for everything means that physical stores are shutting at unprecedented rates. The United States lost nearly one in ten of all its physical bank branches between 2017 and 2021. In the UK, more than two bank branches a day closed in 2021. The digital revolution can be great – unless you're stuck on the wrong side of the chasm. And it can be felt in all parts of life ... including love.

Life and love on the internet

Online dating is big business – and it goes back longer than you might think. While computers have been poring through responses to survey questions to try to find people their perfect soulmate since the foundation of Happy Families Planning Services by Stanford University students in 1959, the first real online dating service in the English language was called the Matchmaker Electronic Pen-Pal Network, which launched in 1986. This used bulletin boards to connect like-minded people looking for love.

The bulletin board eventually became Matchmaker.com, with its own home online. It set the tone for a range of other online dating websites in the early days of the World Wide Web: Kiss.com, launched in 1994, is often considered the first modern dating website, but it was Match.com, which came a year later in 1995, that became huge.

Match was set up by a character we've met before: early web entrepreneur Gary Kremen, who alongside Match.com also owned the much ruder Sex.com. The former was set up with a $2,500 credit card loan and a bold claim: 'Match.com will bring more love to the planet than anything since Jesus Christ.' Within three years, Match.com was worth $6 million, had set up 200 couples who subsequently married – and was directly responsible for a dozen babies. By 1998, half a million people spent $9.95 per month or $60 a year, and 10,000 new members were signing up every week.

Today, Match is just one of many dating services – and its web-based interface seems outmoded compared to the apps that many use to hook up and/or find life partners with. King among the apps, and now owned by the Match Group, is Tinder, which was launched in 2012 at a hackathon held in West Hollywood. The principle behind the app was simple: it echoed flicking through a deck of cards and was designed to seem more like a game than

Exchanging vows online

Seating plans are one of the trickiest bits of any wedding plan. But Stickel and Fuhrman had it all sorted: they'd forego the wedding plan entirely. It was Valentine's Day 1983 and the couple were due to get married. Stickel was twenty-nine, Fuhrman was twenty-three. The couple were set to exchange their vows in Grand Prairie, Texas – but their sixty-six wedding guests were scattered around the United States.

Fuhrman's sister was sat in a Radio Shack in Sacramento, California. Her parents were in Phoenix, Arizona. All were staring at computer screens attached to CompuServe's CB simulator, an early internet chat service named after CB radio. The happy couple wed at their Texas event after the reverend overseeing the nuptials asked Fuhrman, 'Do you, Debbie, take Mike to be your lawful husband?' Fuhrman typed in the words 'I will', at which point the guests' screens flashed '(((((((KISS)))))))'.

seeking a life match. Users swiped left or right, depending on how they felt about meeting up with whoever they saw on their screen.

Within two years, half a billion swipes were happening on Tinder every day, resulting in 5 million matches every twenty-four hours. Now, Tinder makes the Match Group $440 million every quarter, with seventy-five users logging on every day.

And there's evidence that dating apps like Tinder, where you swipe an image right to try to match with the person you like, are becoming more common as a legitimate way to meet your other half. Stanford University's How Couples Meet and Stay Together project takes historical data on how couples got together and augments it with two contemporary surveys, taken in 2009 and 2017.

In 1995, just 2 per cent of couples met online, according to the data. But by 2017, that had become 39 per cent, eclipsing connections brokered through friends (20 per cent) and chance meetings in bars and restaurants (27 per cent).

Happy couples shacking up thanks to an app or their predecessors, online dating websites, may think they're trailblazers – the first generation of algorithmically matched Romeos and Juliets.

But they're not the first ones whose love story featured the internet – not by a long shot. Just ask George Mike Stickel and Debbie Fuhrman (see p. 173).

CompuServe's CB simulator had more in common with the likes of Tinder than you might think. Stickel and Fuhrman's wedding was the world's first virtual wedding, but it was far from the last. Another couple married in Las Vegas, but their ceremony was virtually attended by more than seventy people in 1991. Others didn't marry through CompuServe's chat service but did meet the love of their life there.

The CB simulator shut in 2009 as CompuServe stopped supporting it. Many of the marriages have lasted longer – a testament to true love, no matter how you find it.

Fandom and pile-ons

The uncanny ability of the internet to connect people doesn't just extend to setting up couples; it can also bring together people with like-minded interests, wherever they are in the world.

Fandom isn't a new thing: people have been fans of sports teams for centuries, while popular musicians have had devoted followers for decades. Modern fan culture dates back to dedicated Trekkies, or *Star Trek* fans, who set up mail-based fan clubs and met at conferences for devotees in the 1960s. The prototypical *Star Trek* fandom even managed to save the series from cancellation in 1968, when fans on a tour of the studio backlot where the show was being filmed overheard that the series was not long for the world. They launched a letter-writing campaign that showed NBC, which broadcast the programme, that it had a committed audience.

The television network interrupted programming to ask viewers to stop writing letters, as they had decided not to cancel the show after all.

But fandom en masse was given a jolt with the arrival of the internet.

Suddenly fans scattered around the country and the globe could interact with each other. They could exchange trivia and debate the devotion they had to their interests. And unlike the challenges of organizing a physical letter-writing campaign, internet-based fandoms could pool their collective strength quicker and easier than before.

The collective might of fandom is something to be reckoned with. When singer Michael Jackson died at the age of fifty on 25 June 2009, it immediately became front-page news around the world. But one unforeseen corollary of the pop titan's death was its impact on the internet.

Hollywood gossip site TMZ was the first to report Jackson's passing, and the weight of visitors to the site took it offline. Google – where people turned to search out information about the singer – saw such an uptick in traffic it initially thought it was a malicious DDoS attack, while Twitter and Wikipedia, two sites where people also sought out updates about the death, suffered severe repeated outages. According to one analysis, web traffic as a whole rose by a fifth on the day of Jackson's death as people turned to the internet to find out more. It was an indication of how central the web had become to our world and how we understand it.

Today, some of the strongest fandoms exist in the burgeoning world of K-pop, or South Korean pop music. There, perfectly preened 'idols' (named unironically, for fandoms often put their heroes on a pedestal and worship their every move with a piety religious zealots would be jealous of) are lauded by dedicated fans who organize through platforms like Twitter and Tumblr.

In the world of K-pop, no name is bigger than BTS. The boy band was formed in 2010 and at the time of writing holds at least twenty-three Guinness World Records, including being the most streamed group on Spotify, the most followed group on Instagram and having the most Twitter engagements on average for a music group.

The reason for that slew of records isn't BTS's talent alone – though it's undeniably a major part of their own success. Rather, it's their dedicated fanbase, who have been given the nickname ARMY (not the ARMY, just ARMY) – and act like one, too.

Members of ARMY are slavishly supportive of their idols and can organize quickly and aggressively to correct what they see as misconceptions about their favourite people, even if it's based on fact. As a journalist who has previously written about BTS and its members, I've received death threats and pile-ons from thousands of people who align themselves with ARMY.

They're an example of fandom on steroids, evidencing both the best and the worst of internet-based communities. Their support of their chosen interest is admirable, but it's also full of unwritten (and sometimes written) rules and is waspishly protective against any negative coverage or conversations about the group.

And they're not alone. While ARMY may be the exemplar of fandom, there are plenty of others out there. Swifties support Taylor Swift and congregate in internet chat rooms and around organized hashtags on social media platforms. Johnny Depp fans have created their own unique fandom, doing down Depp's former wife Amber Heard through organized and collective action on social media during the couple's 2022 defamation trial.

Fandom can be a boon. But it also has a dark side.

The world's knowledge at our fingertips

Fandoms never forget slights against their favourites – and the internet more widely never forgets, either.

The internet is a strange beast, simultaneously always mutating and stuck in a state of newness, where the collective memory is shorter than a goldfish's, while also burying deep in its guts an ability to remember more akin to an elephant's.

The short-term memory loss is down to the newness of the whole enterprise. The internet is always adding new websites: Verisign, one of the main providers of domain name registry services, registers 11,000 new domain names every single day.

Many of those contain oodles of new information, while our desire to keep in touch with each other, uploading family photos, holiday snaps or updates to our friends and followers on social networks like Facebook, Instagram, Twitter and TikTok, means that we're always adding to the internet's database of collective knowledge.

Old information is endlessly supplanted with new information, and the constant buzzes and bells of push notifications mean we prioritize what's novel. The internet moves at a clip, with new things arriving every second to grab our attention. And the constant newness has had a negative impact on our attention spans, some academics believe, though the data, and its significance, is disputed.

Yet despite this desire to always consume new information, with fresh content replacing old daily, the internet still has a long memory. In part that's thanks to the great tools of discovery that companies like Google have created, which allow us to search and pull up the internet's entire collective knowledge in an instant. Want to know what people thought of your favourite television show in 2005? Google can provide an answer, digging through the archaeological layers of the internet to dust off contemporary opinions from experts and everyday people alike.

Another tool that can help to unearth the internet's history is the Internet Archive and its Wayback Machine. Founded by computer engineer Brewster Kahle in 1996, the San Francisco non-profit acts as a vast digital library of the internet's sum of knowledge. Much in the same way that you can visit a traditional library and take out a book, so too can you visit the Internet Archive and access huge numbers of copyright-free books, movies and TV shows.

The Internet Archive was Kahle's brainchild, and he laid the groundwork for it deliberately, according to Mark Graham, a colleague and long-time friend of the founder. 'He intentionally became wealthy so that he could build this organization,' Graham tells me. Kahle sold his first company, the internet's first publishing system called Wide Area Information Server, to AOL in 1995 for $15 million.

That might have been enough for most people, but Kahle needed more to achieve his dream. He set up a second company, Alexa Internet, which tracked how many people visited websites on the World Wide Web. That was sold too – to Jeff Bezos for $250 million in 1999.

'He became wealthy so that he could pursue his vision and dream of universal access to all knowledge,' said Graham. The idea for the Internet Archive was simple: 'Could we make available the entire published works of humanity to anyone who was curious.'

The Internet Archive seems like a fool's errand, trying to

capture and preserve information on the internet, which expands at a worrying pace. But it works – and then some.

Going back in time

A secondary project, the Wayback Machine, was created by the Internet Archive at the same time as the non-profit began, but it wasn't unveiled to the public until five years later in 2001. It captures real-time snapshots of websites as they mutate and change, trying to bring a permanence to the impermanent internet.

Since 2015, Graham has been director of the Wayback Machine. It's a fitting role for the former first-class airman with the US Air Force, who set up a prototypical network on the early internet called PeaceNet. It merged with another network in the 1980s to become the Institute for Global Communications, which brought many people online for the first time.

'With the Wayback Machine, we work to identify and preserve material that's accessible to the public via a browser,' said Graham. It's not perfect, he admits, but it tries its best to get its arms around the amorphous concept that is the web and bring a representative sample for permanent storage.

It does that through lists – and lots of them. The Wayback Machine processes more than 10,000 lists daily. Examples include a list of every Wikipedia page added or edited in all 300-odd different-language Wikipedia sites, and URLs deemed worthy of archiving by publishing platforms like Wordpress and content delivery networks like Cloudflare. Individual users can also click a button on the Wayback Machine to archive specific pages they want saved for posterity, too.

As of June 2023, the Wayback Machine had archived more than 817 billion web pages and how they have changed over time, adding hundreds of millions of new web pages every single day to its collective consciousness. As part of its scans of the World Wide Web, it archives new versions of around 1.5 billion URLs every single day, according to Graham.

That might sound difficult – like nailing jelly to a wall – but Graham shrugs it off. 'We're engineers, mostly,' he says. 'If you wanted to approach the problem of nailing jello to a wall, from an engineering perspective, we'd figure it out.' It can sometimes take months or years to work out, but the Wayback Machine does.

It's a boon for reporters and for those seeking transparency, as it helps to catch companies and individuals in lies as they wipe and amend their digital archives. It's also able to be weaponized by fandoms, too, should they choose, by rooting through someone's past statements to find foibles.

But overall it's a tool that's a vital element of accountability online – and one that has made the internet a better, more trustworthy and more transparent place.

How the internet shapes our language

One way the Wayback Machine and the Internet Archive come into their own is in showing how the internet's interests and language is constantly evolving. It's a phenomenon tracked by linguists like Gretchen McCulloch, for whom the shifting sands of how we converse online is an obsession.

For McCulloch, the internet is a rich seam of unfiltered information. From quickly typed-out texts to stream of consciousness tweets, the way we converse online gives a better insight into how we talk – how we *really* talk, when we think no one is really listening – to one another. It's a gold mine full of nuggets that experts in a pre-internet age spent ages trying to figure out how to obtain. And we give it all up for free online.

Aside from the linguistic variations of what people call soft drinks, for example, that are laid bare when you can analyze a geolocated series of missives sent by millions of people, there are more interesting ways that the internet has changed our language – or shown us our individuality. For one thing, the need for brevity on computer keyboards, and later smaller smartphone screens, means that we've taken to chopping down words and phrases into acronyms.

'Laughing out loud' has become 'LOL', or more commonly these days just 'lol' (though its real meaning has changed too, so it no longer literally means audibly laughing). There's also the close cousin, 'lulz', which was coined around the mid-2000s by disreputable forum 4chan, and has a sinister, shlocky side to it.

Similarly, 'IMO' is short for 'in my opinion'. And opinions are something users on forums, and now subreddits, are not shy about providing to strangers.

There are also shortenings that only make sense if you're in a particular subcommunity, some of which occasionally break through into the mainstream. Around fifteen years after it was first coined in 2008, TERF (or 'trans-exclusionary radical feminist', used to describe women who identify as feminists but only on the basis of supporting those who share their sex, rather than gender) has started to enter common parlance, thanks to more mainstream conversations about trans rights.

But it's not just words that have been created or reshaped by the internet; it's also our punctuation. McCulloch has identified a generational gap in the different uses of ellipses (a series of dots like this: …) online. Those whose linguistic norms were formed in a pre-internet era like to separate their thoughts with ellipses because they believe that it helps to identify that they're still talking on an instant message platform and it's not yet your turn to speak.

Yet for younger generations, … can feel like a passive-aggressive action – an eyeroll brought to life and imprinted on your screen. Instead, they're happy to leave the idea that conversation happens in discrete turns to chance, instead chopping up their stream of consciousness into

> separate short missives
> kind of like this
> that act as both a break for breath
> but also as discrete thoughts
> y'know?

Emoji and emoticons

That message above was typed out playfully – not that you'd necessarily be able to tell, which is where emoji (and their older cousins, emoticons) come in.

Spend more than five minutes on the internet and you'll quickly realize it's a linguistic minefield. Whether it's your Uncle Alan waiting to pounce on a perceived slight in your latest WhatsApp message, or a stranger on the internet lingering to pick up on your phrasing in the comment section of a news website, the primary way we communicate online – through the written word – leaves a lot of room for misinterpretation.

Part of the problem is that in the act of writing, you lose huge parts of the nuance of the spoken word. Everything from the tone of your voice to the gestures and faces you make while speaking give the person on the other end of the conversation hints as to any subtext. That subtext is nowhere to be seen in the written word (except when you use dramatic, definitive punctuation like a full stop – the universal sign that enough is enough).

It's something that has been recognized for as long as the internet has existed, which is why humans keen to avoid lengthy arguments quickly developed avoidance strategies.

So people speedily tried to reinject some of that subtext.

Emoticons (a portmanteau of 'emotion' and 'icons') were seen as the answer. And their coming into existence involves a dangerous spillage of mercury in a university lift. Or rather, it doesn't.

It was September 1982 and the Carnegie Mellon University user message board was taking a break from discussing matters of serious import to crack jokes around ridiculous experiments with elevators. Some wondered what would happen if you filled a lift with helium then severed its cable: would it freefall down the elevator shaft or stay floating? Another asked what would change if you put a lit candle and a small amount of mercury in there?

Then – as always – someone took the joke too far. One person added a message to the system: 'WARNING! Because of a recent physics experiment, the leftmost elevator has been contaminated with mercury. There is also some slight fire damage. Decontamination should be complete by 08:00 Friday.'

For those who were in on the joke, it was a good addition. But not everyone was. Some saw the message without the context, and panicked.

The joke was promptly explained, and the conversation turned to how to ensure that confusion didn't happen again. It was the thorny old issue with the written word: it lacks subtle clues like laughter or a raised eyebrow to tip off the recipient that the speaker is joking.

People came up with a number of suggestions, but it was Professor Scott Fahlman who came up with the solution we're all still using (after a fashion) today:

I propose the following character sequence for joke markers:
:-)
Read it sideways.

People did. They liked it. They started using it. Emoticons were born. Variations like ;-) and :-P were created. They spread outside Carnegie Mellon University, and into the world.

The rise of emojis

Emoticons evolved into emojis in the late 1990s, thanks to a Japanese mobile phone company called NTT Docomo, and a graphic artist called Shigetaka Kurita, who designed a collection of 176 pictorial representations of common objects and emotions.

It took until the rise of the smartphone for emojis to become commonly used, and until 2015 for the Oxford English Dictionary to declare an emoji – the crying with laughter emoji – its word of the year, an accolade it was given because it was the most frequently used emoji worldwide.

Chaos and confusion

Until relatively recently, sending an emoji – or, more specifically, certain lesser-used emoji – could be a bit of a crapshoot. Depending on the type of device from which you were sending it and who made the device, and the type of device receiving it and who made it, your carefully chosen pictorial representation of your emotion could look different.

The 'woman dancing' emoji today is comparatively standardized across devices, apps and platforms. It's a woman wearing a red dress, captured in a moment in time mid-salsa, striking her most flamboyant pose. The type of pose differs depending on where it's sent from even today, as do small details: on Apple devices the woman has a grand, ruffled skirt to her dress and red shoes,

	Apple	Google	Microsoft	Samsung
2013				
2014				
2015				
2016				
2017				
2018				

The various ways 'woman dancing' was rendered on different platforms.

while on a Samsung device she wears a hat and rather clunky black strappy heels.

First introduced in 2010, 'woman dancing' was not always a woman dancing. On Microsoft devices, she was for a long time just a grey stick figure. Google showed her as a man.

Nor was 'woman dancing' the only example of an emoji with wildly different interpretations. Most famously, the gun emoji has been changed to some form of water pistol on many platforms but remains a real six-shooter on a handful of providers. It all caused confusion, until the individual tech companies that portrayed emoji drastically differently on their platforms realized that you need (at least) two to tango. So-called emoji fragmentation was causing too much confusion. Starting slowly, the outliers began to meet in the middle, making their icons look roughly the same as their competitors.

Emojipedia, an organization that tracks emoji usage worldwide, decreed 2018 'the year of emoji convergence'. And so, the quick shortcut designed to reduce misunderstandings in missives stopped causing confusion of its own.

Today, the approval of new emoji is a convoluted, bureaucratic process overseen by the Unicode Consortium, the gatekeepers of the emoji. Would-be applicants have to compile a dossier explaining why their chosen icon would be culturally relevant to the whole world; if approved through the first stage, they then submit it to a subcommittee that decides on what emoji to include in annual updates that are implemented by smartphone manufacturers and app makers.

There are now around 3,600 emoji available for users to pepper conversations with – a huge number compared to the 700 or so in 2010. Fearing emoji bloat, the Unicode Consortium has become more judicious in what it accepts: just thirty-one symbols were put forward for potential adoption in mid-2022, roughly a quarter of the 112 approved the year before, and way less than the 334 approved in 2020.

The reason? You can have too much of a good thing. Alexander Robertson, who possesses a PhD in emoji studies from the University of Edinburgh, presented a paper at the Emoji2022 conference in Seattle, Washington. It was a warning from the ghost of emoji future: even adding ten or fifteen emoji a year would mean that by the year 7022, you'd end up with an unwieldy lexicon of 62,000 emoji, or double the average vocabulary of adult English speakers.

GIFs

Another key cornerstone of online communication has as long a history as the emoji: the GIF, an animated series of images that, when looped together, create a short snippet of video-like footage.

Today, GIFs are used to encapsulate complicated emotions in a small space – the perfect example of a picture telling a thousand words. They pepper Twitter threads and forum posts and are deployed in group chats to respond to shocking, exciting or sad news when words simply aren't enough. GIFs are big business, too: in 2020, Meta, the company that runs Facebook, Instagram and WhatsApp, bought Giphy, a giant searchable database of GIFs, for $315 million.

So central to the internet are GIFs that competition regulators in the UK said in 2022 that the blockbuster deal wouldn't be allowed. Giving such a significant Big Tech company like Meta control of Giphy would concentrate too much power in too few hands, the Competition and Markets Authority said. Meta was compelled to sell off Giphy once more.

But before GIFs became tools to communicate clearly and exert power that competition regulators carefully scrutinized, they were something altogether more humble: a way to use pictures online while cutting down on internet bandwidth use and download times.

The year was 1987 – yes, GIFs pre-date the World Wide Web – and early users of the internet were vexed. They had been promised a futuristic-looking communications platform where they could interact with anybody around the world. They'd been told it would be a multimedia platform, where you could interact with images as readily as text. But it wasn't.

Images existed, but the formats in which they were stored and shared were what we'd today call 'bandwidth hogs'. They were big, bulky things that took time to transport across slow internet connections. (At the time, the average internet speed was around 300bps; today, thanks to technological advances, the average internet speed in the United States is 550,000 times faster.) It was like trying to squeeze a three-piece sofa down a narrow hallway: time-consuming, complicated and frustrating.

Now imagine, in that situation, that you're paying the moving company on an hourly basis. Not only do you not have the sofa you want, but you're also losing money in the process. And to make matters worse, the room you want the sofa in is barely bigger than the floorspace the furniture takes up. That was the plight CompuServe customers had in 1987. They were paying an hourly rate for internet access and using computers that had precious little storage space. If they wanted the media-rich, image-led internet they'd been told was possible, they'd spend a lot of time waiting for the file to download – and time is money – only to find they would struggle to make it fit on their PCs.

The GIF's immaculate conception

The problem vexed Steve Wilhite, the forty-something son of a nurse and factory worker from West Chester Township in Ohio. Wilhite was an engineer and computer scientist at CompuServe in the 1980s. He knew images would be important, but he also knew they needed to make them smaller.

GIFs were the answer, but at this time they weren't moving. Theoretically, they could, thanks to a 1989 update to the GIF format overseen by Wilhite, but the data taken up by the image itself limited the ability to repeat frames.

No one knows what the first animated GIF was; some claim it was a cartoonish pixel aeroplane moving across a cloudy sky, others a weather map. But most people can agree on the fact that a major moment in the history of GIFs was when they began to loop.

GIFs today are equivalent to a child's flipbook, where, if you cycle through them fast enough, a series of sequential still images

Crunching down GIFs

The solution to the need for smaller images was a data compression algorithm developed in 1984 by three engineers: Abraham Lempel, Jacob Ziv and Terry Welch. Wilhite came across the engineers' paper, titled 'A Technique for High-Performance Data Compression', and thought it could be put to use crunching down the size of images.

The compression algorithm (also called the LZW algorithm) was pretty intuitive: if it saw repeated instances of data, it would simply smush it all together. In a text file, the computer instruction 'one line break, one line break, one line break' could become 'three line breaks'. In an image, three whole lines of blue pixels marching one after the other, which would have required near-endless repetition of 'one blue pixel' could instead become the much shorter 'three lines of blue pixels'. It's a technique we use all the time in conversation: see '00' in a phone number and you're more likely to say the speedier 'double-oh' than 'zero-zero'.

The LZW algorithm could also blend colours together, creating 'rorange' pixels for red then orange or 'blite' to signify a blue then white one. It was a shortcut. And it saved space. The GIF, or Graphical Interchange File, format was born. (And despite how you might pronounce it, Wilhite is adamant it's said 'jif', not 'g-if'.)

can look as if they're moving. One of the joys of GIFs is that they continue to repeat, endlessly replaying whatever is shown until you close your browser tab or scroll the screen away. But that wasn't always the case. It took until 1995, and functionality introduced by web browser Netscape Navigator, to loop a GIF back to the beginning endlessly.

Under construction

Integration into Netscape Navigator was seminal for the GIF on the World Wide Web. It coincided with an explosion of personal websites being posted on the web thanks to free, ad-supported web hosting companies like GeoCities. Users making their first tentative steps onto the internet seemed to love the idea of having a place of their own online, and so they began building rudimentary websites.

But in the race for newness, they would often publish their sites before they were completed – building their online home room by room and hosting a virtual housewarming before it was all done.

That wasn't a problem, thanks to GIFs, and a series of images that would quickly become synonymous with the early days of the World Wide Web: the 'Under Construction' GIF. Gaudy yellow and black animated GIFs soon became impossible to avoid on the internet. These moving images, which often came accompanied with text explaining that the web page was under construction, borrowed heavily from the signs and cones that road workers and builders would put up around their real-world building sites. They were a symbol of a houseproud, if overeager, new inhabitant of the internet – a message saying, 'I've joined the neighbourhood, but don't worry: I haven't finished furnishing the place yet.'

The 'Under Construction' GIF is a visceral visual reminder for those who were hanging around the World Wide Web in its mid-to late 1990s heyday – almost as immediate a way to transport yourself back to a time and space as the screeching, tinny sound of a 56k modem connecting to the internet through your phone line. And it's one that, despite many of the vestiges of those early days of the web crumbling into dust as early providers disappear (GeoCities closed with a whimper on 27 October 2009), still lives on in some small way.

Internet archivist Jason Scott, who works for the Internet Archive we met earlier in this chapter, decided to try to save this element of the early web for posterity. Before GeoCities shut down its service and deleted all its data, Scott salvaged 959 'Under Construction' GIFs from GeoCities websites that now live on through a website of their own.

Scroll through the page and you'll see a garish, blinking testament to a time many internet users never knew existed – but those who do cherish it deeply.

Long live the GIF

The end of GeoCities, and that early era of the internet, didn't mean the end of the GIF. Far from it. As the internet became more visual and broadband connections meant we could use a broader range of multimedia, the GIF reigned supreme. It has become a major part of our online lives and the way we communicate.

It has moved on from being an odd, meme-like representation to be gawked at, as in the case of the Dancing Baby GIF that captivated early internet users in the mid- to late 1990s. Viewers of the television show *Ally McBeal* will know that the title character would often see a 3D-generated baby wearing a nappy, sashaying from side to side. It was emblematic of one of the earliest memes in the 1990s: the Dancing Baby.

The baby, dancing against a black background, was created using a plug-in to the 3D Studio Max modelling software called Character Studio. Distributed on the internet, others remixed the baby and began emailing it to each other. The Dancing Baby meme was born in autumn 1996, and it remains popular decades on.

In 2012, Oxford American Dictionaries declared GIF the word of the year. It became a main form of communication on websites like Tumblr, launched in 2007, where upwards of 23 million GIFs were posted each day in 2016. The GIF was a central element of posts published on BuzzFeed. It was the subject of a New York museum exhibition in 2014.

The GIF became a standalone response for people on the internet around 2011 according to one academic, who said, 'These brief loops of bodies in motion, primarily excerpted from film and TV, are used to playfully express common ideas and emotions.'

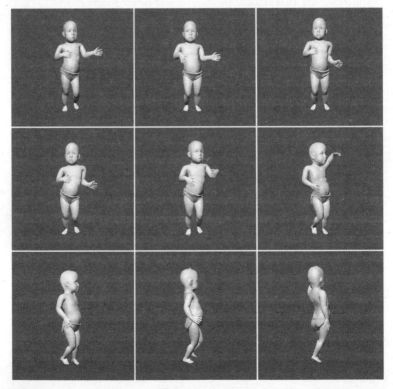

The Dancing Baby GIF. In still form.

And it has outlasted its obituary, which has been written multiple times. Even Tumblr, the platform now most closely linked with the GIF, has previously had enough of it. 'The format is woefully outdated, and this begets massive, low quality animated images,' Tumblr's engineering team wrote in 2015. They would later row back.

Still, it survives. Despite the evolution of high-speed mobile internet allowing us to consume streaming video almost anywhere we are, GIFs remain close to our hearts.

The rise of Netflix

Short, looping video has ensnared us through the rise of GIFs and TikTok and its various copycats, but faster broadband and unlimited data in our connections means that we're just as likely now to sit on our couches and luxuriate with long series and movies delivered to us through the internet. The likes of Netflix, Amazon Prime and Disney+ have all captured our attention, and on-demand video watching has replaced what's now called appointment viewing on television.

But it wasn't always that way. Despite being dominant in the world of professionally produced online video today, Netflix didn't even start online. The company was launched in 1997 as a by-mail movie rental service, from which you could select a DVD to be delivered to your home and replaced with a new one once you mailed the watched DVD back. Within a decade, the mail-order business was starting to wane and home broadband connections were becoming quick enough that Netflix launched an online service where you could watch videos on-demand on computers. The company announced in April 2023 that it would shut down its DVD-by-mail service forever by September of the same year, after shipping more than 5.2 billion DVDs to 40 million customers.

The rise of smart TVs, which were connected to the internet through Wi-Fi and could run apps like a smartphone does, helped push Netflix from PCs onto bigger screens in living rooms. Binge watching whole series of shows through Netflix has now become the norm, and the way that traditional TV programmes are produced and presented has shifted to try to compete with the industry of so-called 'streamers'.

New York Yankees vs Seattle Mariners

Live-streaming video, where video footage is beamed live across the internet, has become a major part of the online experience thanks to platforms like Twitch, where gamers stream themselves playing at all hours of the day. But live-streaming has a much longer history than many might think.

The first live-streamed video on the internet was a 24 June 1993 performance by the band Severe Tire Damage, made up of computer scientists and engineers at Xerox PARC in California. The engineers decided to test out a new technology they had developed which could broadcast a low-quality live video stream over the internet. It proved successful, with viewers as far away as Australia watching on.

That trial was a small one, seen by only a handful of people – but in September 1995 RealPlayer, a PC-based media player, brought live-streaming to a broader audience. It broadcast a baseball game between the Seattle Mariners and the New York Yankees, though only in audio. It would take a few more years for live-streaming video to become commonplace – buoyed by broadband connections enabling better-quality video footage to be distributed online.

The first movie to be premiered online pre-dated Netflix's founding even as a DVD rental service. At 6 p.m. local time on

White and gold or black and blue?

The divisive nature of social media has been made patently obvious in recent years as people have become increasingly and tribally divided along party lines, but the societal ruptures the internet has wrought ought to have been obvious way before Donald Trump was elected president. The reason? Our anger at each other over a dress.

Cecilia Bleasdale posted a picture of a dress she had seen at Cheshire Oaks Designer Outlet in the UK on Facebook in February 2015. It was around a week before Bleasdale's daughter's wedding and she was in the market for an outfit for the big day. She thought the dress might work but wanted to check it was suitable with her daughter. One of the two thought it was blue and black. The other thought it was white and gold.

The image was picked up by journalists at BuzzFeed, where it was propelled through the internet – with each person seeing the colours in the dress differently. It broke the internet, and broke people's brains. In the end, an optical effect accounted for the wild disparity in perceptions of the dress's colour. (Though it's clearly blue and black.)

3 June 1995, Seattle-based web hosting company Point of Presence streamed *Party Girl*, a quirky comedy starring Parker Posey. The quality of the stream wasn't great: the movie's distributor told reporters at the time that it was a fun experiment, but the 'crudeness' of the video shared meant cinemas would remain dominant.

They may have been overconfident. Many Netflix series today have their own dedicated fandoms, tribally arguing over which series is better than the other. The internet has split us. But then we've known that ever since the arrival of a controversial dress on the web (see p. 195).

Never Gonna Give You Up

If The Dress was a sure-fire way to raise the hackles of internet users, there is another cornerstone of the online world that can equally increase blood pressure: 1980s pop star Rick Astley.

For as long as the internet has existed, people have been trying to hoodwink others online. So it is with rickrolling, the practice of sending people a surreptitious link to a video of Rick Astley's 1987 song 'Never Going to Give You Up' when the victim thinks they're being given a link to something else.

The practice emanated from the controversial 4chan image board in March 2007, when one user disseminated links to Astley's song in place of a trailer for popular videogame *Grand Theft Auto IV*. 4chan revels in seeing people being tricked, and doubled down their efforts on April Fool's Day that year. One 2008 survey found that 18 million American adults claimed they had been rickrolled, helping the music video gain more than 20 million views on YouTube by the end of that year.

It took until 2010 for Astley's record label to upload an official music video to YouTube, capitalizing on the song's popularity. Since then, it's been seen 1.3 billion times. Copying the video URL into Twitter shows people continuing to rickroll unsuspecting victims today, claiming the video is actually a trailer for a new *Spider-Man* movie, a YouTuber admitting they were behind the Chinese spy balloon that flew over the United States in early 2023, or a video of football player Lionel Messi supposedly saying he wants to join Manchester United.

Chapter 6
Web3 and the Future of the Internet

A new era

If Web 1.0 was the formulation of the World Wide Web we now use every day, and Web 2.0 saw its consolidation under the control of a handful of Big Tech companies, then Web3 promises to be a break with the old ways and a revolutionary new paradigm for how the web works. At least, that's what its proponents say.

The term Web3 was coined in 2014 by Gavin Wood, computer scientist and founder of cryptocurrency Ethereum, and it was proposed to be something different to the online world we had all got used to. Wood compared the current incarnation of the web to placing all your eggs into one basket. 'If something goes wrong with one of these services, you know, the service is suddenly unavailable for an awful lot of people,' he told a podcast. Internet outages are not unusual as servers or internal processes become misconfigured, as Elon Musk's tumultuous ownership of Twitter has shown us.

Wood's vision was one that was gaining steam among a small section of society focused on cryptocurrencies, the decentralized alternative to money that tech's early adopters believed would overhaul the way we spend. Cryptocurrencies were first invented in 2008 with the release of Bitcoin, developed by a shadowy computer scientist called Satoshi Nakamoto. Although many people have claimed to be the real person behind the Nakamoto pseudonym, including Craig Wright, an Australian academic who has sued people who deny he is Nakamoto, no definitive evidence identifying a single person has been found.

Whoever Nakamoto is published a white paper called 'Bitcoin: A Peer-to-Peer Electronic Cash System' on the internet on 31 October 2008 – a month and a half after the domain name bitcoin.org was registered. The white paper proposed a method of handling financial transactions outside of the banks and tapped into a general distrust of traditional financial institutions; the 2007–08 financial crash was still piling up catastrophe after catastrophe, and most people blamed the banks involved.

The first Bitcoin was minted on 3 January 2009 – a date we know because a reference to a story published by *The Times* was embedded into the code creating it. The headline chosen was clearly deliberate, to punctuate why Nakamoto felt there was a need for Bitcoin:

CHANCELLOR ON BRINK OF SECOND BAILOUT FOR BANKS

The first ever purchase of a real-life item using Bitcoin came on 22 May 2010, when early Bitcoin adopter Laszlo Hanyecz wanted to buy a pizza. He posted on a forum for Bitcoin enthusiasts, offering 10,000 Bitcoin to anyone who would deliver him a pizza. (Back then, businesses didn't accept Bitcoin as standard in exchange for goods or services; today, a small proportion do.)

No one took him up on his offer for days, until nineteen-year-old Jeremy Sturdivant decided to. The two made contact through an IRC (Internet Relay Chat), and Hanyecz sent Sturdivant the 10,000 Bitcoin, then worth around $41. The two large pizzas Hanyecz wanted were dutifully delivered to his Florida home by a delivery driver for Papa John's: Sturdivant had ordered the food online, getting paid for doing so by Hanyecz's Bitcoin.

History had been made – but in hindsight it might have been a foolish decision. While the exchange proved that Bitcoin could be traded for something tangible, which had long been cryptocurrency sceptics' favourite way to downplay the potential of the technology, Hanyecz would have been better off holding onto his investment. As of the time of writing this book, the highest value Bitcoin has hit was in October 2021, when one Bitcoin was worth $66,974.77 – meaning the coins used to pay for the two pizzas back in 2010 would be worth $670 million.

The decentralized web

The core, foundational principle behind all of Web3 is decentralization. The thinking goes that we've spent twenty or more years of our digital lives ceding control of all parts of how we live to tech giants who pump us for our data and then sell it on to advertisers. Those most opposed to the Big Tech business model would say that's been done unscrupulously – though of course the companies themselves say it's all by the book.

For most of us, Web 2.0 was a boon. It broke down barriers to the online world that existed in the niggly Web 1.0 days. Users could log on to most websites with a Google account and pay for items online with PayPal, no matter what site they were visiting. It was simple, quick and efficient.

But that efficiency was a trade-off for allowing private companies more access to who we are – trust that was betrayed, as we discovered in Chapter 3, through scandals such as the Cambridge Analytica incident. It was a Faustian bargain.

We put too much control into the hands of a few central companies who betrayed us. Web3 suggests we never do that again. Rather than giving Google your data or handing over full sections of information about yourself to Facebook, where they can host and control it from their central servers, the idea of Web3 is that all control is decentralized. No individual, or individual company, has a stranglehold on the future of the web. Every user is treated equally and all have the same level of access.

Of course, the information still needs to exist, and it does – but on the blockchain, another foundational element of Web3. The blockchain is a digital ledger, a set of computerized records split into blocks, each of which is verified using cryptographic keys which guarantee its authenticity. You can't change the cryptographic keys, so it's impossible to change history unilaterally on the internet. Copies of the blockchain are stored on different users' devices, meaning that if one person turns up with a version that looks out of sync from the others – because they've altered it, for instance – they can be quickly found out.

That means, for instance, that in the case of cryptocurrencies, any investment can, in theory, be kept safe. But it doesn't always happen that way. Just as bank heists happen in the real world, so too can they happen in the world of Web3.

The world of NFTs

Non-fungible tokens, or NFTs, became massive in 2021, in large part thanks to a series of events that propelled them out of the fringes, into the front and centre of people's attention. Technically, NFTs are a contract and can be attached to anything from bottles of wine to JPEG images, but they quickly became synonymous with artworks, acting as digital certificates of authenticity.

There was the sale of 'Everydays: The First 5,000 Days', an NFT artwork by Beeple, an artist known to his parents as Mike

The Mt Gox heist

Bitcoin's biggest bank at the start of 2014 was a Japanese cryptocurrency exchange called Mt Gox. (An exchange is what it sounds like: a place where you can buy cryptocurrencies using real – fiat – cash, or swap them with other users for other cryptocurrencies.) Seven in every ten transactions that took place worldwide happened through Mt Gox.

Which made its hacking, which was announced in February 2014, and the removal of 740,000 Bitcoins – around one in twenty of all Bitcoin in existence at the time – all the more shocking. By the end of February 2014, the company behind Mt Gox had filed for bankruptcy in Japan and the United States. Those who deposited funds with the company were left out of pocket. And cryptocurrency and Web3 had a big reputational problem.

It's a reputational problem that continues today – and continues to blight many other technologies that use blockchain as their backbone.

Today, many blockchains beyond the one that powers Bitcoin exist for Web3's early adopters to use. One of the best known is Ethereum, the brainchild of Gavin Wood, whom we met earlier and who coined the term Web3, which arrived in the mid-2010s. It is the main competitor for Bitcoin and allows a range of decentralized apps, or dapps, to run. But before Ethereum's launch, there was Namecoin, which was an offshoot of Bitcoin. And Namecoin was home to the world's first NFT.

A collection of Bored Apes.

Winkelmann. That sale, which took place at Christie's auction house on 11 March 2021, changed Beeple's life overnight.

Before he turned to NFTs, the most Beeple had ever made from a single sale of his artwork was $100, for prints of his art. But buoyed by an amazing level of hype – and a fair amount of mainstream media coverage amplifying the sale – one of his NFT pieces was sold for $69 million. That single sale turned Beeple into a titan of the art world: according to Christie's, he immediately became one of the top three most valuable living artists when the gavel dropped at auction.

The reason Beeple's artwork, which was made up of a series of 5,000 images put into a relatively rudimentary collage, fetched such a high price is in part because NFTs were having a moment. A head of steam had been building as obsessives who had become newly rich off the back of ballooning cryptocurrency prices, seeing their initial pennies of investment years ago turn into mind-boggling

How minting works

Minting bears some explanation: NFTs are themselves not the art, but instead are the entry on the blockchain that guarantees the artwork associated with it is the original one. To the chagrin of many NFT investors who didn't understand what they were getting into, it is possible to simply copy and paste the art someone else professes to own and use it somewhere else. But thanks to the immutable, unchangeable way the blockchain works, you can never copy the contract that underpins it – just like an original certificate of authenticity that separates the original Da Vinci from any number of cheap fakes.

</>

sums of money, began using their new-found wealth to speculate on the price of NFTs. Soon, a market sprung up where people bought and sold digital artwork for huge profits.

The hype didn't escape celebrities, who began joining in. On a January 2021 episode of *The Tonight Show with Jimmy Fallon*, socialite Paris Hilton exchanged tips with Fallon about NFTs, including showing each other their own NFTs from the highly popular Bored Ape Yacht Club collection. Bored Ape Yacht Club is perhaps the most well-known NFT collection, with 10,000 images of cartoon apes. It was launched in April 2021 and the organization behind it, Yuga Labs, has been valued at $4 billion. Hilton even ended up gifting everyone in the studio audience at Fallon's show that night an NFT of their own. That hype soon died down – indeed, by the end of 2022 the NFT market had quelled amid allegations that the bubbly traded market was manufactured – but there was a moment when NFTs seemed inescapable, with a new celebrity 'minting' their own seemingly every day.

The concept of minting an NFT was one that didn't exist all that long ago. In fact, 2021's buzzy year of the NFT can be traced back to 2014, when a husband and wife team of artists wanted to sell their digital work.

Jennifer and Kevin McCoy faced the same problem every artist and collector has: proving that the piece they are selling is the original. It's an issue made worse by the ease with which digital copies can be made. They wanted to prove their work, Quantum, which looks like a pulsing star created by computer code, was original. The blockchain provided a solution: they could record its creation in the unchangeable record. The McCoys and collaborator Anil Dash chose the Namecoin blockchain on which to record the minting of the work. It was added to the blockchain on 3 May 2014. NFTs were born.

Of course, that means nothing if no one else follows in your footsteps; the McCoys and Dash had to convince others their idea was worth pursuing. So on stage at a conference in early May 2014, Kevin McCoy sold Dash a different digital image for $4. The ownership was transferred and the blockchain updated.

That paved the way for others to follow. While the Namecoin transaction, and Quantum, didn't last, the trend was set. Around 2017, the first NFTs were released on the Ethereum blockchain, which was far more mainstream and widely used than Namecoin's. CryptoPunks, a collection of 10,000 pixel art characters, were released that year – for free. Those who snapped up the designs ended up sitting on a gold mine, as at the peak of the NFT trading market they were being swapped for millions (the most expensive, CryptoPunk #5822, was sold in February 2022 for $23.7 million).

Blending digital and physical

The principle behind NFTs is a simple one: to blend the digital with the physical. Digital art is worth real money. And it proves the premise of Web3 – there's a way of doing things from a decentralized approach.

All those ideas – the merging of virtual and physical reality, and decentralization – are exemplified in another Web3 technology: the metaverse.

The metaverse was first posited as a potential future right as the first iteration of the World Wide Web was gaining traction. In the 1992 novel *Snow Crash* by sci-fi author Neal Stephenson, the lead character – knowingly titled Hiro Protagonist – is stuck in a dead-end job and seeking an escape. To readers flicking through the book with the benefit of hindsight, Protagonist's lot is eerily similar to theirs.

Traditional money in this new world has been replaced by encrypted digital alternatives. A handful of companies control how the world works for their own benefit, rather than humanity's.

A vision of the metaverse.

(Remind you of anyone?) There is a global economic collapse that leaves most people's lives in tatters. To escape, Protagonist dons a pair of virtual reality goggles and slips off into a digital world called the metaverse, where his digital representation can live a more interesting life.

Snow Crash was written in 1992, but it resonated in October 2021 when Mark Zuckerberg rebranded Facebook as Meta. Those listening to his speech were stuck at home during the coronavirus pandemic as it wreaked havoc on global economies, connected to

Second Life

Hardcore fans of *Second Life*, an online computer game released by developers Linden Labs, have been living in a prototypical metaverse for more than twenty years. *Second Life* was released in 2002, offering an immersive 3D world in which people could live, work and play through digital representations of themselves. (Funny, that.)

And people did. In 2006, when interest in the game was at its peak, *Second Life* had a gross domestic product (GDP) of $64 million and a population of a million users. But it didn't stick. In the UK in 2002, there were just over a million broadband connections to enable the kind of real-time interactions that made *Second Life* a compelling second life. (Today, there are 27 million.) And the graphics were cartoonish, in part because the most powerful commercially available computer microchips of the time had 220 million transistors. Fast-forward to today and the figure is closer to 40 billion. We are in theory more able to leap into this world than ever before. In theory.

each other via social media platforms in the control of a handful of monopolies. The parallels will have been obvious.

Zuckerberg both captured and catalyzed a moment when he pivoted Facebook to become Meta. Nearly 160 companies mentioned the metaverse in their financial earnings statements in 2021, according to financial research firm Sentieo. Some ninety-three of them did so after Facebook rebranded. For good reason: Zuckerberg pledged to spend $10 billion a year to achieve his goal to make the metaverse a reality. He wants a billion of us in the metaverse by the end of the decade.

The metaverse is essentially the world imagined in the sci-fi realm of *Snow Crash* brought to life. Zuckerberg hoped that the metaverse would be somewhere we'd want to live, work and play through digital representations of ourselves. It was connected to the world of Web3 through its fundamental technologies like the blockchain and the idea that we could be wearing clothes bought as NFTs and laid onto our digital avatars.

It was all very futuristic, and the thing that made the time correct right now was the vast advances in internet speeds and computer and mobile phone processing power that we've talked about in the past few chapters. But it also wasn't new – at least not at a high level.

Some of Web3's biggest fans – as well as Zuckerberg himself – believe the metaverse is the future. They see it as inevitable that we'll eventually strap on virtual reality goggles, which allow you to be placed directly into the metaverse rather than see it on a screen, to bank and work and drink and play within that digital world. (Those people are buoyed by the fact that Apple unveiled its Vision Pro mixed reality headset in early 2023, though the $3,499 price tag may put many off.) Others aren't so sure: we had the opportunity to move to a wholly online life during the pandemic when we were forced to stay at home, and

Garry Kasparov plays Deep Blue on 10 May 1997.

when given the chance to socialize in person once more, we leapt at it. Plus, who has $3,499 sitting around to spare on a headset?

This is one chapter of the history of the internet that can't yet be fully written – because we don't know whether the reality of the metaverse will match the hype. But there's one area in the history of the internet which is already being rapidly rewritten and which we can already be pretty certain will have more of an impact than the metaverse could.

Generative AI

Artificial intelligence, or AI, has been around for decades. In 1950, computer scientist Alan Turing developed the Turing test, which he believed would be able to distinguish a computer from a human. British academics in the early 1950s coded computers to learn the rudimentary rules of checkers and chess, while the term 'artificial intelligence' was coined at a workshop held at Dartmouth University in the United States in 1956.

Keyword stuffing

In the early days of search engines, sites would be ranked higher in the results if they were seen to be more relevant to what users were searching for.

They work on the basis of keywords. If you were looking for recommendations for a new car, you might search for the phrase 'best new car to buy'. You'd also likely want to find 'good new automobiles' and could well search for popular marques like Ford, Vauxhall, Chevrolet, Fiat and Volkswagen. You might search for terms like 'best miles per gallon' or 'most reliable car'. So if a site wanted to rocket to the top of search results, they'd load their pages full of these phrases.

Keyword stuffing was born. The content wouldn't always be hugely useful – in fact, it often wasn't because the site's content was written, usually by cheap, outsourced labour, to include as many keywords and phrases as possible without necessarily thinking of making the writing lucid. And it flooded the internet with garbage web pages. Some even buried great lists of keywords and phrases in the same colour as the background of their website, in tiny text in footers to try to game the system.

AI continued to develop over the coming years, with key milestones including Deep Blue, a computerized chess AI, beating then human world champion Garry Kasparov by analyzing 200 million potential moves every second before deciding on the right one. But Deep Blue's knowledge was comparatively shallow.

And it would take a little while longer to get to the AI age we're currently living through.

People got rich on servicing the needs of businesses and individuals looking to rank higher on search engines. Google eventually got wise to keyword stuffing and changed the signals that dictated what made a high-ranking site. But those wanting to populate the site still had to pay people to make the content.

Generative AI, which was becoming mainstream in 2023, doesn't need that. Instead, it can do it all itself. Ask it to produce 500 words on how to change a car's carburettor, and it'll generate the text. It won't be perfect, and it might not make sense if you read deeply, but it'll be there.

The idea of being able to produce screeds of text with little more than a simple sentence to prompt the generative AI model, which 'learns' to write by inhaling vast volumes of text from the internet, was propelled into the public consicousness by the release of ChatGPT by San Francisco company OpenAI in November 2022. The beta release of the tool became so popular that it repeatedly crashed. Investment bank UBS estimated that 13 million people used it daily, asking it to do their homework, to produce an episode of *Friends* as if written by William Shakespeare or to generate copy for their website.

Here's what happens, by the way, if you ask ChatGPT to write an episode of *Friends* in the style of Shakespeare:

Title: 'The One with the Midsummer Night's Dream'
[Scene: Central Perk. **CHANDLER**, **MONICA**, **ROSS**, **RACHEL**, **JOEY**, and **PHOEBE** are sitting on the couch.]
MONICA: Pray, Chandler, what maketh thou of yonder crossword?
CHANDLER: A challenge, dear wife, a challenge. Yet with thee, I

feeleth invincible.

[RACHEL enters, looking distraught]

RACHEL: Ah, woe is me! My heart is heavy.

ROSS: (rising) What has befallen thee, sweet Rachel?

RACHEL: I have been passed over for promotion at Ralph Lauren.

ROSS: Fear not, dear Rachel. Thine opportunity shall come.

PHOEBE: Or mayhap it's a sign to follow thy true calling, just as the Fates have written.

RACHEL: And what might that be, sweet Pheebs?

PHOEBE: Hmm, I know not. Something with unicorns, mayhap?

JOEY: [confused] Unicorns? In New York?

(Enter GUNTHER, carrying a tray.)

GUNTHER: More coffee, good sirs and fair ladies?

ALL: Aye, Gunther!

(They all laugh.)

ROSS: (to Chandler) Say, Chandler, didst thou make any progress with that joke thou were crafting?

CHANDLER: Why, yes. Prithee, how do you call a man with a seagull on his head?

ROSS: I know not, how?

CHANDLER: Cliff. Get it? Because it's a sea ... gull? On a ... cliff?

[All groan.]

MONICA: Methinks thou needst more practice, my love.

RACHEL: (stands up) I shall to the restroom.

[Enter JANICE, Chandler's ex-girlfriend.]

JANICE: Oh, my God!

[All gasp.]

JANICE: (to Chandler) Didst thou miss me, my love?

CHANDLER: Zounds!

[End of Scene 1]

Whatever you think of the punchline it provided in Central Perk, ChatGPT was unlike anything else users had ever seen. It was a large language model (LLM), trained on a vast corpus of text gathered on the internet. It had consumed the world's knowledge – and appeared eerily able to converse with people about any topic, to put itself to any task asked of it and to answer any question posted to it. AI and chat-bots are twin technologies that have been hyped as the future for years – but with ChatGPT, it finally seemed like the future had arrived.

You might be able to see where this is going. Whereas the low-quality content that typified the worst, most inaccurate corners of the web used to take time, money and human labour to produce,

Deep learning

Artificial intelligence had long been trained to tackle specific tasks, but it wasn't able to put more generalized knowledge to the test when presented with something outside of its immediate area of expertise. Put Deep Blue, which beat a chess grandmaster, to work trying to write an outline for a new reality TV show and it wouldn't know where to start. Humans set the tasks, and the computer complied. It didn't ever try to learn, really. It would just replicate.

AI needed to be more conniving. And in 2014, a group of academics came up with a way to make that happen. In June that year, researchers at the University of Montreal published a paper titled 'Generative Adversarial Networks' onto the arXiv, an online server that hosts academic research. Ian Goodfellow had coined a phrase – and developed a concept – that would come to revolutionize the AI age and leave footage generated by the likes of now it can be done in an instant by AI. It's early days, but this could prove fatal to the web, as high-quality, human-generated content drowns in a sea of AI text.

Deepfaked images

It's not just text that generative AI, which works by spotting patterns in work it is trained on then making linkages between concepts it sees to try to 'understand' its world, can be deployed to create. Images, audio and video can all be AI-produced.

And that comes with complications. It means that increasingly people online will encounter AI-generated content – which more

Video Rewrite or the Active Appearance Model looking like a child's drawings compared to a painting by Picasso.

Generative Adversarial Networks, or GANs, pit two 'neural networks' against each other. Massively simplified, these networks think a little like how our brains do. They are trained on vast volumes of data, so you could train a neural network on images of politicians, for example, until it becomes expert at depicting them.

One network in the GAN is called the generator, and its job is to make fake content based on what it has been trained on. The other network is the discriminator. It tries to catch the generator in a lie, to tell real creations apart from fake creations. The two play a game where each tries to beat the other, simultaneously improving what each of them does. Eventually, they get good enough at their tasks to develop work that's virtually indistinguishable from the real thing.

cynical minds could call inauthentic. Some of that content will be innocuous. Some of it will be dangerous. All of it should be carefully checked for blurriness, odd ears or extra fingers, in case it changes your mind.

The early 2020s saw a slew of so-called deepfake content (where AI and other tools are used to generate images that don't represent the reality, or skew it in such a way as to be misrepresentative of what someone actually said or did), but the concept dates back a lot longer.

The first innovation in deepfake tech came in 1997, when Christoph Bregler, Michele Covell and Malcolm Slaney, three engineers at a company called Interval Research Corporation, released an academic paper and computer program they called Video Rewrite.

Video Rewrite used pre-existing footage of a person to automatically create new video of the person saying words they didn't speak. It analyzed how the person's mouth moved in the original video, matching it to what they said: an 'oh' sound would see the mouth make a perfect circle, or an 'ee' would show them stretching their lips wide across their teeth. The mouth images would then be reordered to mimic the movement of someone's lips saying something new. The researchers thought it would be ideal for movie redubbing.

The concept was refined and advanced by other academics, who developed a technology they called the Active Appearance Model, or AAM, in 2001. It used computer vision and algorithms to more smoothly match up sounds and facial expressions. But it took the development of deep learning artificial intelligence to really make the convincing images we'd now describe as deepfakes.

How AI changes search

The world of search has remained largely the same since Google became the giant gorilla in the room in the 1990s. Google remained dominant despite others trying to muscle in, constantly updating the underlying technology behind its search engine in order to maintain its supremacy. In February 2011, it unveiled Google Panda, which overhauled the way Google ranked results to show in its searches so as to try to head off those trying to play the system with low-quality search results.

The year after, it introduced the Knowledge Graph, contextual information about whatever a user is searching for that meant they didn't need to click away to a page. Updates came regularly after that, but they were small steps rather than giant leaps.

Microsoft, comparatively, has languished behind in the search engine wars for years. Following the launch of ChatGPT, however, it saw an opportunity. It took a $10 billion stake in OpenAI in late January 2023 and unveiled a new version of Bing, powered by a souped-up version of ChatGPT, on 7 February 2023.

Google, spooked by this, reacted. Realizing what was going on, it tried to spoil Microsoft's party, unveiling its own LLM-based search tool, Bard, a day earlier. After years of stagnancy, the search war was back on.

Chat-based search powered by AI is a revelation, and a step change in how we understand and navigate the vast amounts of information online. (It has parallels with the early web search engine Ask Jeeves, but this time it is truly interactive.) Rather than being presented with a list of links to click through to find information, the information is combed through and presented to you, with the opportunity to interrogate the AI 'brain' about all it has learned. But there's just one problem: it often makes things up – a bit of a problem when talking about the search for facts.

One AI researcher, Julian Togelius at New York University, compared it to Sigmund Freud's early work dissecting electric eels to try to find their life essence – without success. Freud was a superb thinker and destined for greatness. But in his early days he was casting around for an outlet for his talent. Adding AI to search is similar to that, Togelius said: 'If you try using them for dissecting electric eels – producing factual answers – you're kind of wasting your efforts.'

Still: Big Tech companies are trying. At the time of writing, Microsoft and Google are trying to convince more of us to migrate to chat-based engines. Whether it sticks will have to wait for the next retelling.

The future?

AI, GANs and Web3 all promise to overhaul the way the web works – and with it, rewrite the rules of the internet. It puts enormous, powerful tools into the hands of people who haven't previously had them. Chat-based generative AI allows us to outsource large parts of our thinking to computers – a potential boon for our creativity and the broader economy.

The image, audio and video generative AI tools at our fingertips have the potential to drastically elide the creative process and vastly improve our productivity. Some believe that generative AI will be a wrecking ball for creativity, while others see it as an eager assistant, enabling them to spark more inspiration. It can allow new artwork to appear from nowhere in an instant and for people to produce professional-standard work without any effort.

Those who have seen the long run of the internet and technology's history say this moment we are living through will be one of the defining times of the internet era.

But every silver lining has a cloud behind it.

Just as the web in its earliest days was filled with clickbait and keyword-chasing nonsense designed to hoodwink hungry search engines rather than produce worthy information that could benefit browsers, so there are concerns that the rise of tools that make creating content easier could end up filling the internet with detritus.

In the vast landfill of information that we have already formed in the thirty-odd years of the web, there are worries that we're backing up truckloads of generative AI work to pile on top. What happens next is unknown. We've never been in this situation. The generative AI tools we're now using to make new content are themselves trained on the internet's vast corpuses of information. There's a worry that we're sleepwalking into a world where we create a twenty-first-century ouroboros, the ancient serpent devouring its own tail.

There's a saying in AI: garbage in, garbage out. The fear is that if we swamp the web with generative AI-created content, which in turn is used to train the next generation of tools, we end up losing objective fact. We end up losing the human essence of creativity. We pile the rich archaeology of the internet with artificially generated rubbish and submerge the good stuff so deep it can never be discovered again.

Is AI the brilliant, shining future of our lives just around the corner, or a funhouse mirror reflecting the worst elements of our society back at us in a grotesque caricature? It could certainly have helped to do a lot of the initial sifting of the internet's timeline for this book, for one thing. But it would also require plenty of oversight to make sure it didn't make catastrophic errors. Nor, hopefully, could it have written as engagingly as I have.

Acknowledgements

Trying to summarize decades of internet history into readable, comprehensible chunks is tricky. My thanks go to Angelika Strohmayer for acting as a lay reader, pointing out where a draft went far too techy and bringing it back to basics.

Thanks too to Vint Cerf, one of the fathers of the internet, for granting us the ability to print an excerpt of his poem, memorializing it, and to Mark Graham and Leonard Kleinrock for talking to me about their memories.

And thank you also to Glenn Fleishman, who kindly offered to look over a draft of the book and provide a technical review, making sure I haven't made any catastrophic errors – though I hope readers forgive any that have slipped the net.

The facts contained within this book come from a collage of sources, including a number of books written about various parts of the history of the internet and World Wide Web, alongside documentaries, newspaper clippings and archive footage from the time events took place.

Picture Credits

Every reasonable effort has been made to identify the copyright owner of the images used in this work. If nonetheless a credit is incorrect or has been omitted, please contact the publisher with details and we will rectify as soon as is reasonably possible. Contact details are found on our website. Thank you.

Index